DESIGNER PRIMER

FOR ARCHITECTS, GRAPHIC DESIGNERS, & ARTISTS

TOM PORTER AND SUE GOODMAN

Butterworth Architecture

London   Sydney   Singapore   Wellington

Acknowledgments

The authors would like to thank the following people for their encouragement and help in providing material and information for the production of this book:

Michael Alfano, Juan Carlos Calderón, Richard Crenshaw, George Dombek, Will Fay, Philip Jones, Larry Lowic, Thorbjoern Mann, Tom Martineau, Piccola Randolph, Linda Roach, Ronald Shaeffer, Peter D. Stone, Edward T. White, and Bill Wiencke.

Special thanks are also due to Richard K. Chalmers, Enn Ots, and Judye MacCalman for making it possible for Tom Porter to visit the School of Architecture at Florida A. & M. University, Tallahassee, and conduct experimental graphic workshops with many of its students.

The drawings on page 28 showing the front page of the January 24, 1987 issue of The Times are published with the permission of The Times Newspapers Limited.

First published in 1988 in USA by Charles Scribner's Sons
This edition published 1989 by Butterworth Architecture, an imprint of Butterworth Scientific

PART OF REED INTERNATIONAL P.L.C.

British Library Cataloguing in Publication Data

Porter, Tom
  Designer primer: for architects, graphic
  designers and artists
  1. Drawings. Techniques
  I. Title II. Goodman, Sue
  741.2

  ISBN 0-408-04318-0

Library of Congress Cataloging-in-Publication Data

Porter, Tom
  Designer primer

  Includes index.
  1. Graphic arts--Technique 1. Title
  NC1000.P665 1988 741.6   88-6550

Printed and bound by Hartnolls Ltd, Bodmin, Cornwall

TABLE OF CONTENTS

Introduction

In the wake of a rapidly advancing computer-graphics technology, drawing by hand remains undisturbed as the central activity in the process of design. Design ideas, it seems, are still conceived of using pencil or pen on paper. Indeed, this is confirmed by a recent survey of design practices. The survey found that, compared with a computer literacy, management and modelmaking skills, etc., an employee's ability to draw both in freehand and with drafting instruments--in that order--was of paramount importance.

Therefore, the central theme of Designer Primer is its commonsense approach to objective drawing and design drafting for beginners. Chapter 1 examines the act of drawing as an extension of our visual perception, i.e., as the creation of spatial illusion on a flat surface. The understanding of the difference between what we see and what we think we see is then developed in Chapter 2. Here, pictorial images are dismantled and analyzed in terms of their constituent working parts.

Drawing mediums are discussed in Chapter 3 and evaluated for their sketching capabilities. This section serves as a prelude to a matter-of-fact approach to objective drawing techniques in Chapter 4--a section that also includes a variety of useful methods for achieving accuracy in the drawing process.

The functions, spatial prowess, and drafting techniques specific to each orthographic and design drawing type, as well as to composite versions, are reviewed in Chapter 5; alongside these are projects intended to harness design concepts to graphics and develop design drawing techniques. Finally, Chapter 6 focuses on the creation of professional-looking and visually compelling graphics, and on the all-important issues of their individual production time.

The word "artist" rarely appears within the text. Drawing in all its forms is explained step-by-step in the conviction that an understanding of how and what we see--with both the eye and the mind's eye--is the foundation of an honest and convincing drawing technique.

VISUAL PERCEPTION

Sensations of Space

1

As we move through space, each body, neck, and eye movement sets the visual environment in motion. Of all the sense organs, the eyes receive by far the most spatial information. The physiology of the brain indicates that the visual scanning process is capable of monitoring up to eighteen separate images every second.

Our perceived experience of environmental space is primarily a sensuous event involving movement, for to pass through an environment is to cause a kaleido-scope of changing impressions, of transitions between one spatial sensation and another. Each experience affects the orchestrated functioning of our senses in a variety of ways--our eyes, ears, nose, and skin registering changing stimuli that trigger a flood of brain responses on all levels.

2

However, touch is an important aspect of our understanding of space. The psychologist Sven Hesselgren has outlined three tactile dimensions. The first is the actual sensation of physical contact with the surface of an object.

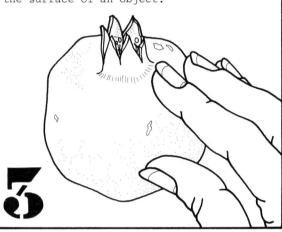

3

The second tactile dimension is experienced when we pick up an object. In holding it we gain an immediate impression of its weight--this sensation being recorded by the kinesthetic activity of our muscles, which make infinitesimal adjustments to the balance of our body.

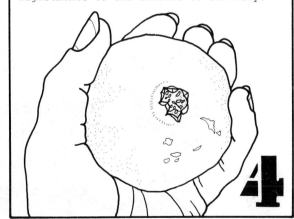

4

If we close our eyes, using our hands to explore the entire surface of an object, we experience the third dimension of touch--a haptic percep-tion of its form. This sensation is the most reliable of our sense organs in acquiring knowledge of the exis-tence of physical form.

5

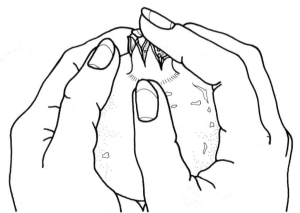

Sensations of Space

6 Despite the importance of vision and touch, we should not ignore the distance receptors, such as hearing, in relation to the acoustic properties of space--for example, the way in which the sound of a footstep informs the brain about the volume of a reverberant room.

7 Smell is another distance receptor and is an aid in identification and orientation. For example, a hungry person will screen off other senses to enable him or her to find food using a more acute sense of smell.

CAFÉ

The use of perfumes and colognes and the Colgate toothpaste "ring of confidence" is a further example of screening in a society embarrassed by body odors and bad breath.

8 This screening out of other senses in order to concentrate on particular sensations is common, such as when we close our eyes when listening to music or during lovemaking.

9

10 Being more subtle in their sensitivity to temperature, humidity, texture, and shape, the immediate receptors (skin, membranes, and muscles) are sensitive to movement.

Oriental designers accentuate this kinesthetic aspect of our tactile appreciation of space by a manipulation of irregularly positioned objects, such as in paving. Walking through such a space necessitates an increased and correspondingly irregular number of muscular sensations.

The Visual Field

1

The world around us is seen by our eyes within a circular-shaped format called the field of vision. The range of this visual field is extensive. For example, if you hold your arm fully outstretched to one side and at right angles to your line of sight, it is possible to detect your hand at the outer reaches of your vision-- especially if you wriggle your fingers. Located at the very center of the visual field is the very clearest viewing zone. This occurs immediately around the point at which our two eyes converge to focus on a point or object in space. Situated around, and especially to each side of, this clearly focused area is the progressively unfocused ring of peripheral vision. This monocular zone is perceived by each eye independently, and as we approach its outer limits, the detection of movement, such as that of your moving fingers, becomes more effective than the perception of an object, such as the shape of your hand.

The limits of the inner, binocular (or two-eyed) visual field is horizontally more than 180 degrees and vertically more than 130 degrees. However, within this area lies the sharpest and most accurate zone of the entire visual field. This is the central cone of vision, which ranges from 30 degrees to 60 degrees both horizontally and vertically. Within this central cone of vision the range for accurate shape and symbol discrimination is 30 degrees, and depending upon the quality of the viewing condition, colors can be discriminated accurately in a field extending out to 60 degrees.

N.B.: The shaded regions at the top and bottom of this diagram represent the almost unnoticed intrusion of the eyebrows and the nose on the hazier outer limits of our peripheral vision.

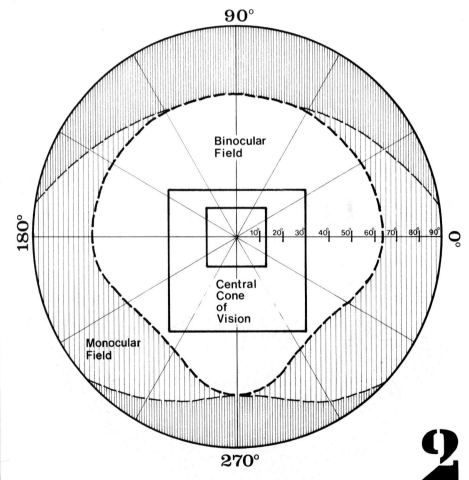

2

The Cone of Vision and Sight Size

If we project the most accurate and distortion-free segment at the center of the field of vision, we form the cone of vision, i.e., a beam of sight that has its apex in the eye and whose conical projection registers everything clearly within a 60-degree angle on the horizontal and vertical planes.

The cone of vision shifts and adjusts with every movement of the eyes as they fixate on points in the distance and points close at hand. However, if we draw events that lie outside the range of a fixed cone of vision, we encounter distortion. The equivalent of this graphic distortion is not experienced in the dynamics of normal vision because we are continuously refocusing to accommodate new information in the field of view.

As the size of objects is conditioned by the proximity of the viewer, so, too, is the size of the drawing. For instance, the nearer the viewing position, the larger the object will appear and, consequently, the larger the resultant drawing. Conversely, the more distant the view, the smaller the resultant perception and, indeed, the drawing.

In photography, the telephoto lens comes closest to human vision. However, the distortion seen in this photograph results from the "cone of vision" of a fish-eye lens, which demonstrates the effect of a view exceeding 100 degrees.

In order to avoid problems of on-the-spot rescaling, it is important to begin drawing at the size at which the subject is seen, i.e., at sight size. Sight size is easily understood if we imagine the size the subject matter would assume if seen on paper as though through a sheet of glass. Drawing at sight size allows for measurements to be taken directly within the scope of the field of vision.

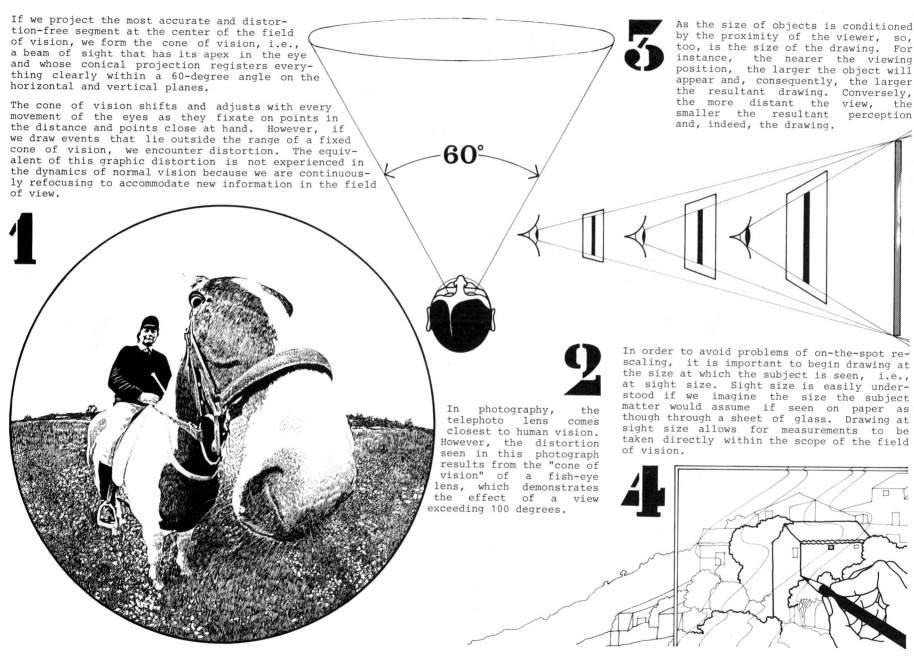

60°

Binocular and Monocular Vision

The primary visual signals or cues that aid our perception of objects in space are binocular vision and motion parallax. Binocular vision, i.e., two-eyed vision, can be divided into three component but related parts: disparity, accommodation, and convergence.

Disparity describes the fact that each eye receives a slightly different image from a stimulus. For example, we experience disparity if we line up a distant object with a vertical line, such as a window glazing bar, that is just a few feet away. Then, as we close and open each eye in turn, the vertical line will appear either to the left or to the right of the distant object.

LEFT   RIGHT

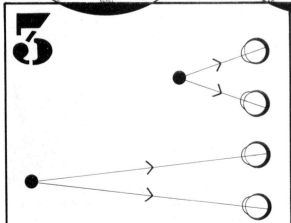

Accommodation is the ability to focus our eyes on only one point at a time. For instance, when we concentrate on the distant object, our impression of the glazing bar dissolves. Conversely, when we focus on the glazing bar, the distant object loses focus.

Convergence is the angle subtended by the two eyes on the object in focus--a nearer object subtending a larger angle, a more distant object a smaller angle.

Our eyes give overlapping fields of view and stereoscopic depth vision; motion of the head and eyes gives motion parallax, in which farther objects move less, such as the relative movements of nearer trees and distant hills when seen from a speeding train.

Apart from holograms, stereoscopic images, and moving pictures, all forms of graphic display are monocular. However, we always look at images with both eyes and often walk about in front of them. This experience of motion parallax works against the illusion of depth, as we are immediately aware of their flatness.

How the Eye Scans Images

When we look at a scene, the eye cannot focus on more than one very small point at any one time. This tiny point of acuity exists at the center of the much wider field of vision. Visual data received outside the focused center of vision become progressively less determinate as they range out to the blurred outer reaches of our peripheral vision.

Therefore, a scene is never viewed "at a glance"; rather, it is reconstructed via a scanning sequence in which the eye flits continuously from point to point to complete an almost instantaneous visual reconnaissance of the situation.

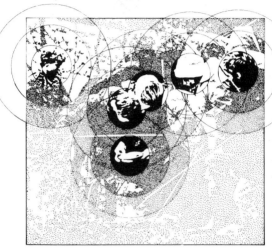

Similarly, when we scan familiar objects, places, and scenes, such as the view through a window, we take in little detailed information. As contrast and change induce perceptual arousal, familiarity with the stimulus breeds a jaded and casual appraisal.

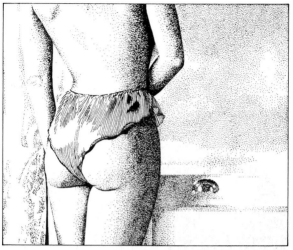

Visual scanning is an issue-oriented operation, i.e., people with quite different motives and interests will view the same scene in quite different ways.

Studies confirm that people in the Western world tend to scan bland arrays of pictorial information in much the same way as they read text, working downward and scanning from left to right. In this initial scanning review, images take precedence over written material, and large images tend to attract the eye before smaller images.

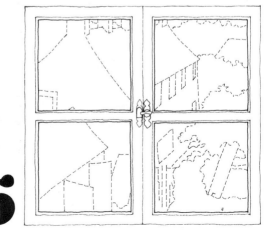

Conversely, observation drawing--and, indeed, foreign travel--heighten our level of sensory perception. For instance, if we were to make a detailed drawing of the same familiar window view, this demanding experience would induce a sharpened seeing process--a superimposed succession of slow-motion and searching scans of the view's details.

Single-Glance and Switched-Foci Graphics

1

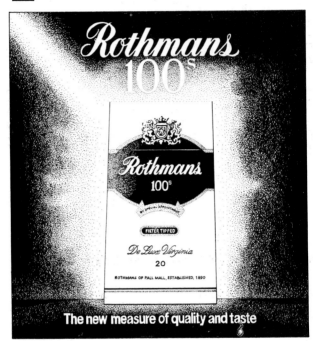

2

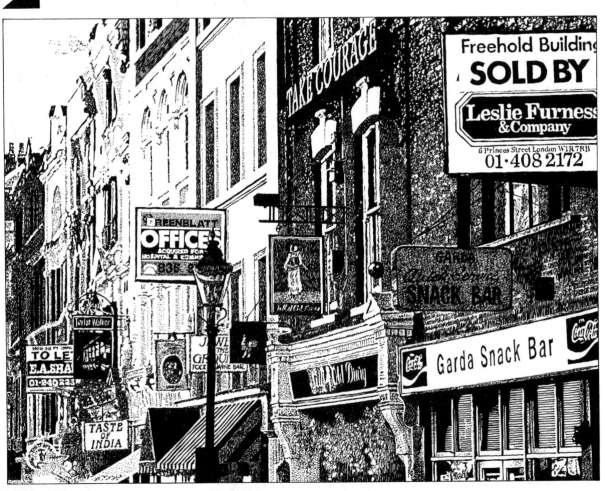

Pictorial displays seem to respond to the nature of our field of vision in two basic ways. One is the single-glance graphic, which usually contains a single point of focus. It presents information apparently seen--and intended for rapid visual consumption--in a single fleeting moment. Such graphics range from quick sketches to ads (often absorbed from the "corner" of the eye) to French Impressionist paintings, the last portraying a diffuse impression of the behavior of light on objects with one central point of focus.

Single-glance graphics simulate a fixed, momentary view of our field of vision in which the area of sharp focus--representing a stationary point of convergence of our two eyes--is surrounded by a blurred outer edge that reflects the gradual diffusion of information into the region of peripheral vision.

By contrast, in switched-foci graphics, the total area of the pictorial display is evenly in sharp focus. Rich arrays of detail invite a close encounter with all regions of the format and, in stimulating eye movement, provide the wandering eye with high degrees of information. Perhaps the best example of this type is Pre-Raphaelite art, which filled large canvasses with meticulously painted detail, such as landscapes in which every blade of grass is "seen." Although structured within a fixed cone of vision, such drawings and paintings respond to the voraciousness of our eye and induce it to make a searching journey around their formats.

Multiglance and Motion Simulation

Both examples of pictorial images on the facing page respond to a fixed cone of vision and its corresponding field of view. However, there is another, rarer form of graphic that, in using a dynamic cone of vision, takes in the wider information of a multiple viewpoint. The resulting fusion of vision causes distortion. An example of multiple-viewpoint imagery can be found in the work of artist John Bratby, whose changing field of vision often encompasses not only the subject matter at his center of vision but also views of parts of his own body in relation to it.

This drawing is taken from John Bratby's painting "Window, Self-Portrait, Jean, and Hands."

1

2

Yet another form of distortion results from attempts to simultaneously record a variety of angles of view of the same object. Pioneered by the Cubist painters, such graphics stem from the movement of the viewer about the three dimensions of an object in order to communicate its total understanding. This approach necessitates the fragmentation of glimpses for their graphic reassembly into a single image.

The illustration is based on a painting by Georges Braque, "Musical Forms 1913."

3

However, beyond graphics that are created from fixed or moving cones of vision, there are those that--despite being denied motion parallax --attempt to simulate the motion of objects across the field of view. These range from reducing the moving object to a blur, or indicating "echo" lines behind its trajectory, to dismembering the object into serialized views of its movement through space. However, movement can also be simulated in gesture drawing (see page 53).

Gestalt: Similarity and Proximity Grouping

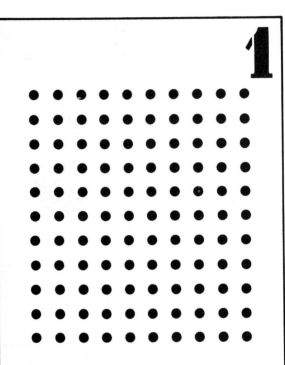

1

The Gestalt theory also proposes that the eye has a facility to absorb only a limited number of unrelated elements. For instance, when confronted by too many dissonant elements, the eye, in failing to construct a unified image, tends to reject its impression as disorganized and chaotic.

2

3

At this point it is worth touching on the work of the Gestalt psychologists, who studied the act of seeing as a dynamic and creative process involving both the viewer and the viewed. Their theories have stressed that--in seeking harmony and unity in visual information--our perceptual system first sees a "gestalt" (image) as a unified whole before identifying its constituent parts; furthermore, that our tendency to initially group things into simple units is governed by unit relationships, such as proximity (the relative nearness of elements to one another) and similarity (the relative sameness of elements). For example, the regularity of the dot configuration in this classic perception demonstration causes the eye to search continuously for a stabilized and unified resolution. In so doing, the eye scans the ordered arrangement of identical elements, constructing and reconstructing a changing but unresolved sequence of rows and squares.

Again, when the same units are rearranged into a new configuration, the familiar shape of a cow is recognized before we become aware of both its constituent elements and their regrouped arrangement.

4

However, when these same elements are reassembled into related family groups of shape, their newfound qualities of "sameness" and "nearness" appear less disorganized.

5

Being based on our past experience of images, the phenomenon of visual grouping is demonstrated by the way we continuously search for pictures--even with minimal data. We can reconstruct faces in a fire and in the marks of wood grain. Visual image-building stems from the mental grouping of elements with like characteristics, such as size and shape. For example, the sliced edges of circles in this detail from a Vasarely painting are quickly grouped to form a connected line.

Gestalt: Similarity and Proximity Grouping

6

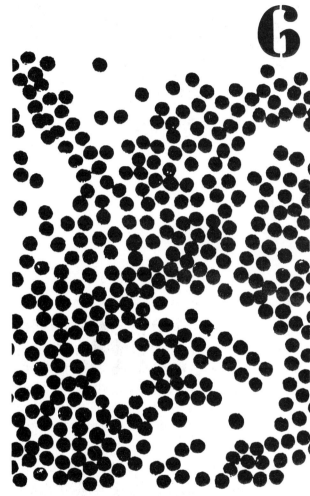

7

The visual bonding of elements due to proximity takes place at particular points in their juxta-position. Providing the units are close enough, even dissimilar elements will be grouped.

Although the eye and brain can construct images from limited data, the resolution of the perception will remain incomplete if too many bits of information are missing from the stimulus.

8

Another interesting aspect of visual grouping is our perceptual facility for closing, or "painting in," incomplete information. In this image, the eye prefers to reconstruct the ghost of a white triangle rather than accept the two families of shape.

Therefore, in order to reassemble a comprehensible graphic, a resolved "gestalt" relies upon an adequate number of visible clues being present in the stimulus.

However, when elements are of the same size and shape, the character of the grouping process will rely upon proximity between the elements—a quality conveyed by the amount and type of interval between them. This is one of the late Maurice de Sausmarez's student projects in which each dot symbolizes a person in a crowd of soldiers and rioters. Discrimination between soldier and rioter in this abstraction is quickly made by a visual assessment of their spatial relationship to each other.

9

10

The Basic Axial Structure

Research using the Eye Movement Recorder—a sophisticated apparatus for tracking the movement of the eye over two-dimensional visual information—has established that the eye and brain make an initial scan of visual matter to determine the basic equilibrium, or balance, of an image. This is established when the location and relationship of the main horizontal and vertical forces within the image have been identified. Recognition of this underlying structure is important because it functions as the backbone of a composition. These basic axial forces are also embodied in both regular and irregular shapes contained within the image—their balancing vertical and horizontal axes being easily sensed.

You can practice the isolation of these basic axial force lines by studying different magazine photographs selected at random. First, draw a horizontal line through each photograph to summarize where you think the main lateral thrust occurs. Follow this by drawing vertical lines to represent each major perpendicular axis. The point at which the axes intersect usually defines the key area of a composition, i.e., the visual fulcrum, or center of balance, that is unique to each image. It is important to be aware that the axes may not coincide with lines or edges in the photographs. Rather, each is a linear summary of the key massing and its placement within the format.

Some images may contain a whole series of horizontal and vertical axes that reflect a hierarchical structure of grids that underline a more complex or intense distribution of information.

Primary and Secondary Scanning

In her book A Primer of Visual Literacy, Donis A. Dondis discusses the results of research that has identified two phases of rapid scrutiny in the scanning of pictorial material. During the initial scan, the eye sweeps essentially from left to right in its search for the whereabouts of the main vertical and horizontal axes.

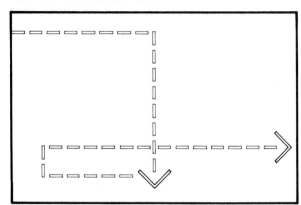

This almost instantaneous survey is then followed up by a secondary sweep, which brings the focus of the eye to rest momentarily in the lower left region of the format.

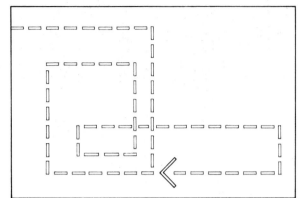

According to the findings of this study, it is in this lower left sector of a graphic that the eye expects to find the dominant message.

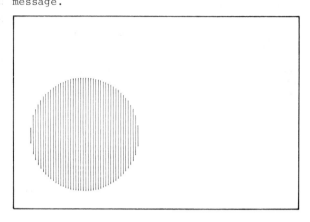

In this selection of ads from a single magazine, the main message area of each format is located in a zone that seems to respond to the expectation of the scanning eye. Whether or not these graphics were designed in direct response to an awareness of our lower left preference is an open question, but a large proportion of the other ads in the same magazine tended to use this area of the format for their message.

BP Oil

Dunhill King Size

Leveling and Sharpening

1

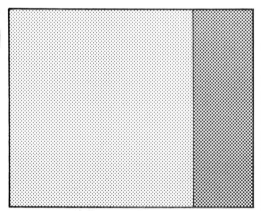

According to Dondis, the visual axes of compositions divide formats into areas of information that are capable of presenting different degrees of challenge to the eye. For instance, when the lower half of a graphic holds dominance over the upper half, this relationship of emphasis makes for a stress-free, or (in psychological parlance) "leveled," compositional response. The fact that an inverted arrangement of emphasis appears more stressful possibly stems from its challenge to our learned experience in the natural landscape.

Also, when the left-hand side of a graphic exerts dominance over the right-hand side, we locate emphasis in the region where the eye expects to encounter information. **2**

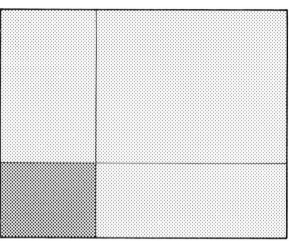

Furthermore, when we draw the eye into the lower left region of the format, we create a maximum stress-free leveling, as this area represents the natural resting place of an information-gathering eye. **3**

4

On the other hand, when the right-hand side of a composition embodies more visual emphasis than its left-hand counterpart, we begin to build in a degree of perceptual surprise, if not anxiety, which is termed "sharpening." This response occurs because the eye is less prepared to encounter information in this general region.

5 However, when the full weight of emphasis is located in the upper right-hand area of the format, we create the sharpening effect of maximum stress and surprise.

6

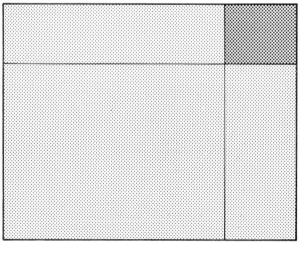

Dondis suggests that this preference for the left in compositions corresponds to a dominantly right-handed Western society that reads from left to right but physically tends to fill up rooms--such as restaurants-- from right to left. Leveling and sharpening also extends to our response to degrees of irregularity and complexity in shape. However, a basic working knowledge of the potential eye-pulling attraction of visual information when placed in different areas of the format holds enormous significance in compositional design.

A Biological Balancing Act

1

In his book The Biology of Art, Desmond Morris records some fascinating image-response tests with apes. Armed with a pencil, the apes revealed remarkable compositional tendencies. Here are just a few of the findings:

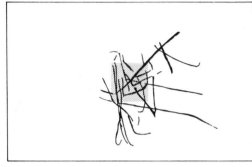

When confronted with a sheet of drawing paper premarked with a central square--either in value or delineated--the chimpanzee subject almost consistently produced a tight concentration of marks in the region of the figure.

2

When multiple figures were presented, the chimp would recognize both their presence and the close proximity of their grouping by scribbling connections between them.

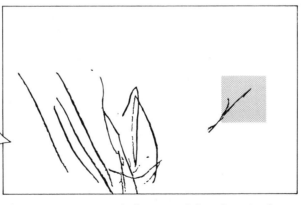

This tendency to balance, although not always acted upon, occurred when the figure was offset--either to the left or to the right of the format.

3

However, in further tests when the positioning of the two figures began to define a central space too large to ignore, marks were made as if to fulcrum the two figures.

Furthermore, responses to true balance were made both in the horizontal axis and in the vertical axis.

4

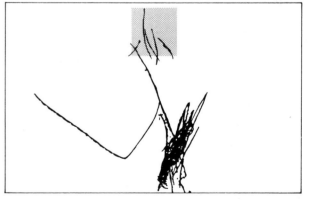

5

Symmetry and Asymmetry

Similar response tests using offset squares but this time with human infants found very similar reactions. The search for balance in composition seems to be the same in both children and chimpanzees.

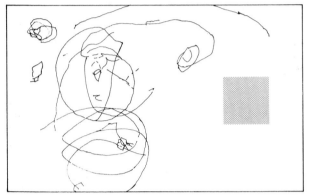

1

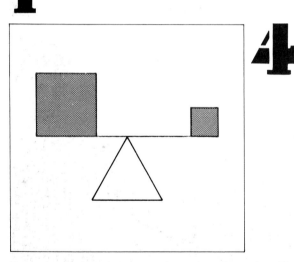

Extreme asymmetry creates tension in the viewer and can be used to good effect in attracting the eye. The unequal size and differential location of elements around a focal-point fulcrum create an interesting example of asymmetrical balance.

2

Both appear to innately assume a central axial fulcrum with a surrounding distribution of weight on either side. However, perfectly symmetrical, or centered, arrangements can appear predictable and unprovoking.

4

However, asymmetrical balance derives from equal eye attraction. Here, this is achieved using a small focal point whose importance in the composition is amplified by the directionality of the larger supporting shapes.

There is another form of graphic equilibrium that is achieved by balancing elements of unequal weight and dissimilar size. For instance, this drawing provides a counterbalance of differing areas of value to achieve an alternative visual equilibrium.

3

6

5

As highly variegated areas of texture and pattern offer more interest to the contrast-seeking eye, small areas of heavily textured information can be used to counterbalance the asymmetry of larger, less textured areas.

Perception vs. Representation

1 All forms of graphics are illusionistic versions of our understanding of reality. For instance, when we make an observational drawing, we translate what we see into a form that will fit into the flatness of the drawing surface. To do this we also have to learn to see in terms of the marks made possible by the mediums, such as ink and graphite, that we use. To accomplish this transformation, we have to suppress our knowledge of the familiar meanings of objects and events in order to transfer them as lines, shapes, and values to the imaginary picture plane. Therefore, the act of drawing involves the application of a new set of meanings--a detachment that, historically, has led to mechanical measuring devices, such as this grid contraption seen in Dürer's woodcut "Draftsman Making a Perspective of a Woman."

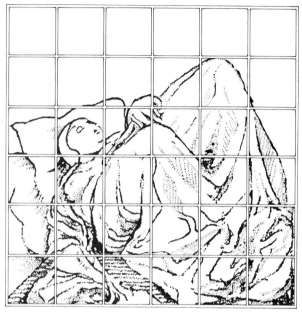

If we enter the space of this drawing and peep through the draftsman's gadget (a glimpse reconstructed by Betty Edwards in her book <u>Drawing on the Right Side of the Brain</u>), we see his foreshortened view of the model fragmented into a mosaic of squares. The function of the grid has been to act as an intermediate filter between the draftsman's knowledge of the human form and its analytical reduction into flat, manageable units of graphic information.

2

In his book <u>Art and Illusion</u>, E. H. Gombrich states that we are rarely prepared for the actual relationship between the size of objects when they are projected onto the picture plane. For instance, if we were to trace a window view directly onto the pane, we would encounter surprises, such as the diminutive size of drawn distant objects compared with our perception of them.

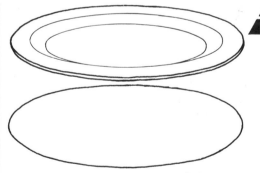

4 5

The difference between our understanding of objects and their representation is demonstrated in an experiment conducted by H. Thouless, who tested the perceived sideways view of a plate with a series of graded ovals. In each case, his subjects tended to overestimate the roundness of the perceived plate by matching it with an oval exhibiting less foreshortening. In other words, their knowledge of its roundness caused its perception to be greater than its retinal size.

The conflict between perception and its representation is highlighted when we make accurate prototypes of the sizes of objects within our field of vision. For example, the difference between perceived foreshortening and a photographic version is due to a modifying mechanism known as "constancy" (see page 26).

Rectangular Conditioning

1 One aspect of the way we view our surroundings is the conditioning effect of our environment. Culturally, we live in a rectangular world --a world defined by buildings and objects characterized by straight lines and corners. Overexposure to this kind of setting has meant that our vision, being continuously bombarded with rectilinear information, has developed a subtly conditioned and specialized perception.

2 A by-product of this conditioning is that our visual perception can be made to experience optical illusions. Optical distortions such as this are common in our perception of the modern environment, as in the visual warping of straight lines and in the upward thickening of tall buildings.

3 Also, when decoding two-dimensional images, we are unable to "read" certain shapes as being flat. Here is a collection of shapes that our perception refuses to accept as being flat.

4

The ancient Greeks were fully aware of optical illusions, because, in embodying no straight lines in its structural elements, the designers of the Parthenon anticipated the visual warping of large-scale parallel lines.

In comparing primitive and sophisticated perceptions, the scientist R. L. Gregory describes the world of Zulu tribesmen. Theirs is a curvilinear culture, with dome-shaped huts entered through circular openings and filled with rounded furniture. Gregory explains that Zulus do not experience the optical illusions common to our perception. Our specialized vision is also underlined by anthropologist Anthony Forge, who describes how New Guinea tribesmen could not interpret photographs, as they had not learned how to decode graphic information.

Optical Illusions

1

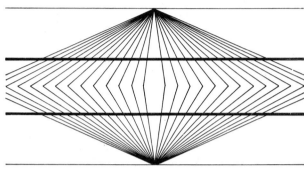

Others, such as the Müller-Lyer Arrow Illusion, are not in themselves distorted but produce that effect when viewed. Although the line above appears to be longer than that below, the two are equal in length.

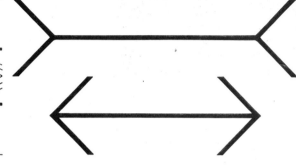

There are many different types of optical illusion, the image of which the eye and brain find difficult to resolve. There are two basic kinds of illusion. Some, such as Wundt's Illusion, rely on the effect of a background pattern to cause distortion.

A further type of illusion is the equivocal figure whose three-dimensional message can be reversed by the eye. Schröder's Staircase is just such an illusion, for it can be viewed at will either from below or from above.

2

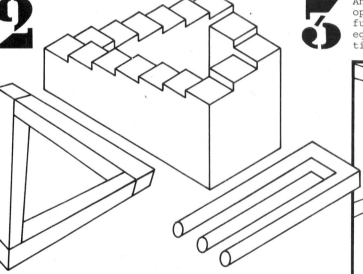

3 Another type of illusion simply and optically dazzles the eye and confuses the brain by a discharge of equally weighted positive and negative information.

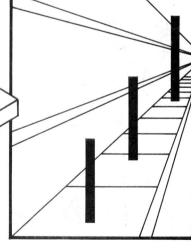

6

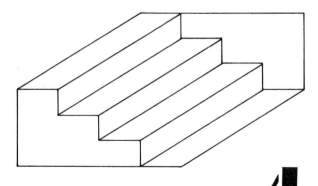

4 5 Irrational figures fall into another category of visual illusion. These convey credible information about the form of an object that, in reality, could not exist outside graphics. Optical illusions such as these cannot be explained in terms of reality, because reality and perception do not correspond.

However, in his book _Eye and Brain_, R. L. Gregory demonstrates that optical distortion is related to our perception of depth, and that when perspective features in figures increase, a greater degree of illusion results.

Optical Illusions and Theories of Vision

1 In human vision, the eye translates the reality of solid objects into two-dimensional images that are then converted into a pattern of symbols in the brain. In this sense, our vision works in the complete reverse of photography.

Studies by Hubel & Wiesel of the visual cortex of the monkey's brain have shown that the brain does not respond to light as such, but to sharp features, such as edges and lines.

For example, compare these two areas of value before placing one finger on the central division and making a second comparison. The difference between the two comparisons is possibly due to the eyes' detecting the sharp central edge in the first view and "painting in" two shades of gray. Once this edge has been removed, the second view sees the grays as similar in value.

Other research suggests three stages of vision. First, the eye converts an image into boundaries and shapes.

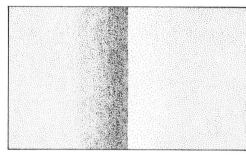

2 **3**

4 **5**

Furthermore, optical illusions demonstrate that this process can come up with the wrong interpretation, such as in Fraser's Spiral. In this illusion the brain miscalculates the given information and "sees" a spiral where no spiral exists.

Second, the brain then makes assumptions during the reconstruction of the shapes into likely three-dimensional shapes.

Third, the brain arrives at a full three-dimensional picture of the objects in view.

Optical Illusions and Theories of Vision

6

Another theory of vision proposes that our brain carries a "file" of familiar objects against which the signals received by the eye are compared. Being intolerant of ambiguity, the brain, in receiving information from this illusion, plumps for one image--the profile of a young woman--or the other image--the head of an ugly hag. In seeking a familiar object even when confronted by an unfamiliar shape, we can alternate between the two mental hunches.

The figure is based on an illusion designed by E. G. Boring.

7

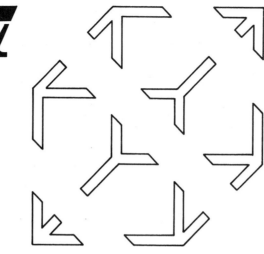

A further example of the way in which the brain is apparently programmed to construct three-dimensional images is seen in this curious comparison of two drawings. In the first we see only separate shapes . . .

. . . but in the second we see a cube seemingly masked by "invisible" white stripes --the brain simply enclosing the incomplete image to reconstruct a solid form.

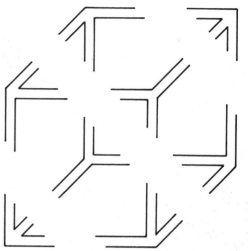

8

9

Apart from color, there are probably three levels of information being processed simultaneously in the brain: form, distance, and motion.

Information concerning form is easily recovered by the brain. For example, when we look at an unfamiliar picture composed entirely of shading, its signals are quickly and easily converted into three dimensions.

Constancy Scaling

1 A further factor must also be accounted for if our representation of space is to be congruent with our perception of reality--the phenomenon of constancy, i.e., the difference between the image that enters the eye and the same image as reconstructed by the brain.

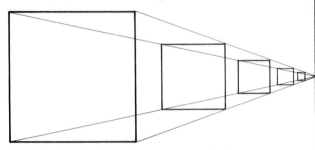

As an object increases in distance, it follows the law that its size will halve with each doubling of the distance from the viewer. However, this law refers to the retinal image and does not account for the zoom-lens capacity of the brain, which compensates for the shrinkage of objects.

2 This is the phenomenon known as constancy and can be experienced easily by holding one hand near to the eyes and the other away at arm's length. Although their retinal image (for example, that recorded by a camera) would show them as quite different in size . . .

3 . . . their perceptual size as modified by the brain would be quite similar and apparently little affected by distance.

4 The comparative effect of constancy scaling with the "retinal" image of a camera and that of a measured perspective was carried out by the authors in Oxford's market. This image represents the "retinal" image of a photograph.

5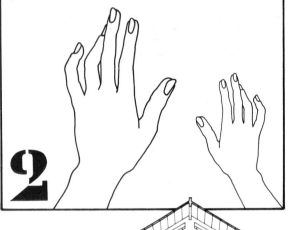

This is a measured perspective drawing of the same space, made from the same point. As in the photograph, constructed perspective bypasses the constancy effect.

6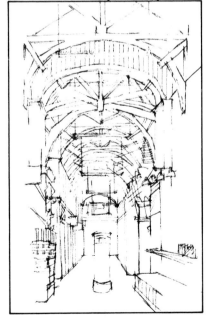

By contrast, the modified eye and brain image of a student free-hand sketch allows the effect of constancy scaling to have impact. Notice that the back wall plane appears nearer the viewer--the brain having modified the perception of the space.

2 UNDRESSING PICTORIAL IMAGES

Three Layers of Perception

1

As we move about the space of our environment, the amount and nature of visual information we receive are regulated by our distance from the stimulus. This relationship between distance and type of information can be classified into three degrees of perception. For example, if we view the front page of a newspaper from afar, we are more aware of its primary elements, such as its format, layout, title, headline, and lead picture. In contrast to the size of these primary elements, all remaining graphic signals appear diffuse and subordinate.

2 If we move closer to the page, a secondary layer of information comes into view. This new perception includes smaller illustrations, ads, captions, and other graphic devices, such as bullets and rules. Also, what appeared in the initial view as gray blocks now take on the potential of columns of text.

3

Our final step toward a third encounter with this newspaper reveals a rich layer of highly detailed information that presupposes an ability to read the text. These three viewpoints can also be translated into degrees of interest and commitment. For instance, in the first view, interest is casual; in the second, it is half-committed; and, finally, in the third, it is fully committed to the stimulus through reading the text.

The Primary Graphic Elements

If we were to continue our perceptual zoom in on the newspaper on the facing page and make a microscopic examination of one of its photographs, we would discover that its image is comprised entirely of colonies of minute printed dots. A network of spots of varying size, number, and proximity can be interpreted by the eye as connected by invisible force lines that, when reassembled visually, allow recognition of identifiable images.

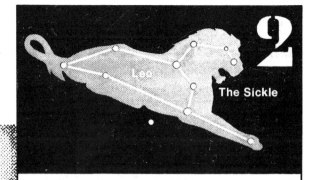

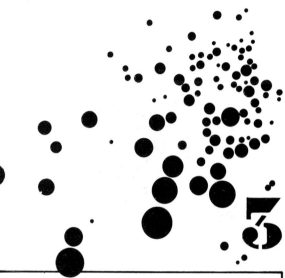

Similarly, when dots of different size are spontaneously scattered, a greater variety of energy and tension is released which, apart from the pattern of movement, infers depth and space in the visual field.

The dot introduces us to the most basic graphic element. Having no scale, it signals an energy point within the visual field, like a star seen in the night sky. However, the patterns of meaning associated with astronomy result from our star-gazing ancestors, who, experiencing the proximity tensions of closure, translated the clusters of pinholes of light into delineations of animals and objects.

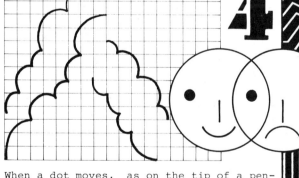

When a dot moves, as on the tip of a pencil or a pen, it becomes a line. This is the most common graphic element. Lines signify directional energy capable of transmitting emotional connotations of aggression and stability. Upward curves elicit a sense of cheerfulness, while their descending counterparts register a corresponding emotional slump.

When a straight line loses stability and control, its zigzag pulsation assumes an emotional electricity that has attracted the attention of psychologists and the more scientific artists, such as Victor Vasarely.

Whenever we connect the two ends of a line, the contained area assumes a concept of shape that is perceptually detached from the surrounding area; this figure-ground phenomenon relegates the line into subserviency.

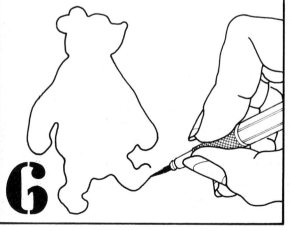

The Primary Graphic Elements

7

In graphics, the figure-ground phenomenon concerns the visual alternation of what is considered positive, or solid, with what is considered negative, or void. In drawing, the recognition of negative shape is important because the shape of space surrounding form is just as "positive" in the visual field. This interdependency is demonstrated in this classic reversible figure. For instance, if we fix our gaze on the central white vase, the surrounding areas--represented by black--appear to define its form spatially. However, if we switch off to a concentration on the outer areas (the two black face profiles), we discover that what was seen as "negative" transforms into a positive but different entity that takes on a life and a meaning of its own. In this second perception, what was at first void has now become tangible--the vase-to-faces alternation causing a graphic experience of negative shape as a dynamic presence, being redefined by the same contours that had previously described the vase.

The term "negative space" refers to the three-dimensional depth, the volume of air or empty space within which the solid volumes of a picture are organized behind the picture plane.

8

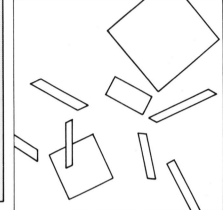

10

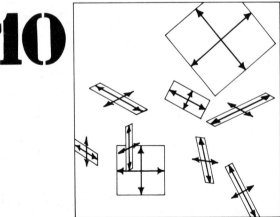

Both regular and irregular planes generate their own tensions along their long and short axes. When planes are parallel to the picture plane, they are seen as being static and two-dimensional. However, when planes are tilted or rotated away from the picture plane (and, therefore, the viewer), they are seen as dynamic and three-dimensional.

The picture plane is the flat, two-dimensional format represented by the drawing surface. Within and behind the imaginary space of the picture plane, shapes can occupy different planes. However, the picture plane will always remain at right angles to the line of view.

9

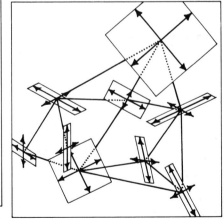

11

Therefore, any worthwhile pictorial image will represent an underlying organization of a whole array of different tensions that are generated by the apparent spatial interplay between the surfaces of the assembled planes.

The Primary Graphic Elements

12

The most basic planar figures are the square, triangle, and circle. These represent a family of shapes embodying vertical, horizontal, diagonal, and curvilinear relationships. However, faced only with outlines, we have no means of determining their respective volumes.

The volume, i.e., the amount of space occupied in three dimensions, of the triangle and square becomes apparent only when we have visual access to their cross-sections; but the circle, being the same from every angle, remains ambiguous. Therefore, we have to introduce a tonal modeling in order to fully realize its form.

13

14

Value is a most important element in graphics because, apart from signaling direction of light, textural nature of surface, and position in the depth of space, it controls the underlying structure of achromatic artwork. Furthermore, together with hue and chroma, value is a vital dimension in the structuring of color schemes.

This is a drawing based on an etching by Aldo Rossi.

16

There are two types of texture in graphics: tactile and optical. Essentially, tactile texture is what is experienced via the sense of touch. Therefore, strictly speaking, tactile texture in graphics is the surface quality left behind after the application of mediums. Popularly defined, however, it means a literal depiction of a surface.

Optical texture refers to the creation of visual surface effects. In drawings, lines or dots describe tonal value, but their textural grain will also describe an optical texture-- an effect that may or may not be incidental to the image being communicated. The experience of graphics is simultaneously modified by a supplementary experience of all the graphic elements. In other words, value is color, color is form, form is texture, etc., etc., for we perceive each as a facet of all the others. This illustration is based on the work of Roy Lichtenstein.

15

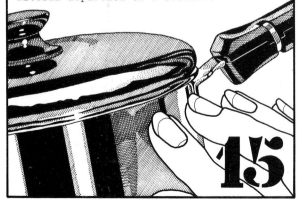

Undressing a Two-Dimensional Image

2 Let's begin our analysis by simply differentiating the figure-ground relationship, i.e., the linear separation of the proportion (mass) and negative (spatial) areas (A). To extend this figure-ground analysis, we can now identify the three basic pictorial zones. These comprise foreground, middleground, and background (B). In a further stage of our undressing sequence, we strip back the image to a line that contours both the number and location of its basic forms (C). This delineated rawness can now be fleshed out using a searching line to describe every discernible shape in the picture. If meticulously worked, this analysis discloses a complex pattern of shapes that combine to form the basic network of the image (D).

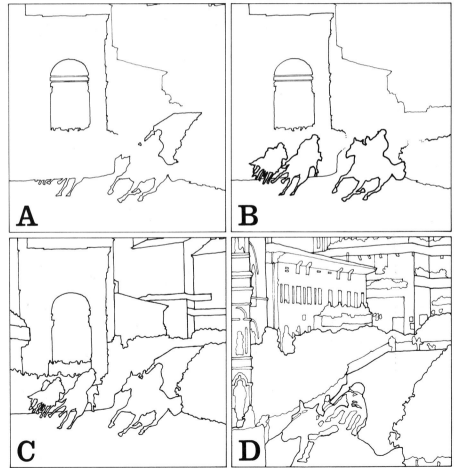

1 Most two-dimensional images--including those in design, art, and the media--comprise a visual cocktail of signals that are superimposed over a less obvious underlay of structural information. In order to understand how some of these signals work, we should learn to visually "undress" a pictorial image by peeling away some of its constituent elements. The following frames represent just a few of the countless ways that, through the technique of visual analysis, we can isolate the ingredients of an image. This kind of graphic striptease act is useful not only because it helps us to understand the nature of the seeing process, but also because it aids our understanding of the act of image-building.

Undressing a Two-Dimensional Image

This same linear pattern of perceptual patches can also be translated as a complex network of tonal values that, in either the original scene or its photographic version, reflect color. Each shape in this network of pattern contains a specific value that, to a greater or lesser degree, differs in tone from that of its neighbors. If we look carefully at the nature of the resulting pattern, we find a fascinating and unpredictable structure of interlocking shapes. A close scrutiny takes us to the very guts of our graphic, for this is the essential diagram of patches that is perceived by the eye and translated by the brain into the illusion of space.

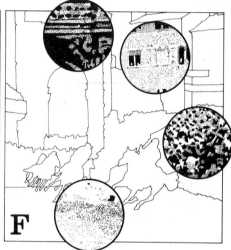

The incidence of this pattern of values responds, in turn, to the amount and direction of the light source. We can now isolate this vital ingredient by recording exclusively the precise shapes of only the shades and shadows (E). If we now turn to the basic delineation of shapes that define the number of formal elements in the original, we find that each presents textural attributes that communicate a range of environmental surfaces. This analysis isolates and identifies a selected number of differently sized planes and shapes that occupy different locations in the illusion of space of the original photograph. Various types of surface quality are indicated, such as rough, smooth, glossy, matte, specular, etc. (F). Without such information our original image would appear a uniformly dull event with little or nothing to be seen.

Dismantling the Depth Signals

1

Another means of understanding the mechanics of an image--but this time in relation to the illusion of depth--is to dismember a graphic into its constituent number of depth cues. However, before so doing we must reinforce the fact that the following depth cues relate to a fixed monocular (or one-eyed) vision. This is because all two-dimensional images are seen without the stereoscopic ability of a binocular (or two-eyed) vision and also without the means of making comparative depth judgments between two spatial objects by using head movements.

Overlap is a simple but most efficient depth signal. It describes which objects are closer and which objects are farther away. It also helps us identify the relative location and scale of objects.

First, the relative size of objects in our format indicates both depth and scale. However, in order to make a depth and scale assessment we have to base our decision on a known object, such as a human being.

2

Another aspect of aerial perspective is the gradual diffusion of edge and detail over distance. Such comparisons associate sharpness with "nearness" and blur with "farness."

4

Aerial, or atmospheric, perspective is a depth signal that uses the progressive haziness of values and/or colors as they lighten or become more gray with increasing distance. This is shown if we isolate a piece of foreground and compare it with a piece of background.

3

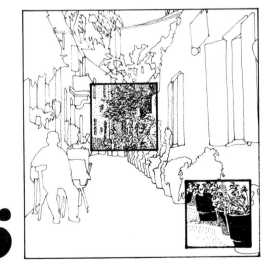

5

Dismantling the Depth Signals

Linear perspective is a spatial system in which parallel horizontal lines appear to converge as they recede and meet an imaginary line called the "eye level" or "horizon line." When extended, all the parallel lines on each vertical plane converge on common points, known as "vanishing points" (see pages 38-39).

The position of an object within the frame of the picture is another strong means of assessing spatial location. For instance, the higher an object, the farther back it is assumed to be.

Diminishing interval between equally spaced objects is another powerful indication of depth in both the horizontal and the vertical planes.

In creating shade and casting shadows, the incidence of light in our image is a vital depth cue. If we carefully study its effect, we can see how its projection represents an amalgam of all other depth signals.

We can test this graphic cue by looking down into the space in front of us. What occurs closest to our feet is lower. As we lift our gaze, objects progressively higher in the field of view appear as farther away.

Finally, the scale, size, and location of signals indicating textured surfaces will, by their comparison, strongly influence our impression and judgment of depth in the illusion of our two-dimensional image.

Graphic Depth Perception

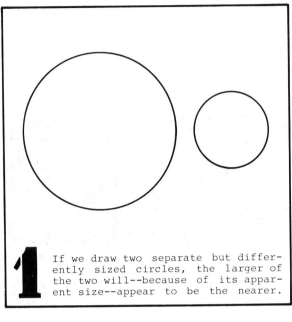

1 If we draw two separate but differently sized circles, the larger of the two will--because of its apparent size--appear to be the nearer.

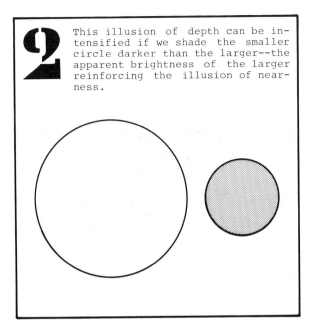

2 This illusion of depth can be intensified if we shade the smaller circle darker than the larger--the apparent brightness of the larger reinforcing the illusion of nearness.

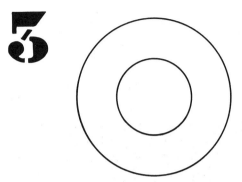

3 If we redraw the two circles with the smaller inside and at the center of the larger, the resultant space becomes ambiguous--a visual conundrum caused by the lack of depth cues. For instance, does this image represent inner space (a microscopic view of two blood corpuscles); outer space (a planet passing its sun); interior space (a view down a tube); exterior space (a plan of a hat or a doughnut); or nonphysical space (a diagram of the Colgate "ring of confidence")?

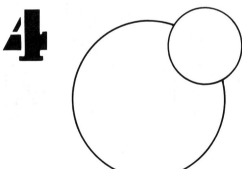

4 If we again redraw the two circles but this time with the smaller partially overlapping the larger, a more powerful depth cue operates, reversing the first impression. The idea that a portion of the larger circle is hidden by its smaller counterpart instantly informs the eye of a new juxtaposition: the hidden area has not ceased to exist, it has simply been removed from view, with the resulting implication of a certain distance existing between the two objects.

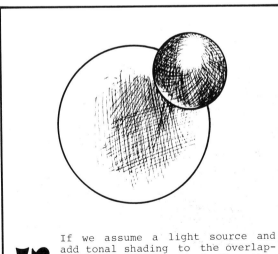

5 If we assume a light source and add tonal shading to the overlapping circles, we can further this illusion of depth. However, even this seemingly convincing picture can be ambiguous.

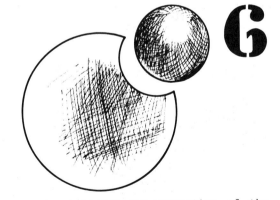

6 We can again challenge our perception of the apparently overlapping circles by applying a more complicated yet feasible answer: that the larger circle now exists in front of the smaller--the latter being viewed precisely through a cutaway portion of the former. J. J. Gibson employed just this visual trick in his famous experiment designed to determine the relative importance of the various cues to depth (see facing page).

Two Classic Depth Perception Experiments

An interesting test studying the comparative effects of size and brightness on our perception of depth involved two partly inflated balloons, each illuminated from concealed light sources and positioned 10' (3m) away from observers.

When the size and brightnesses of both balloons were kept the same, observers saw them as being equidistant from their point of view.

When the size of the two balloons was kept the same and brightness altered, nearly all observers considered the brighter of the two balloons to be the nearer.

When the brightness of both balloons was kept the same and the relative sizes were changed, observers considered the larger balloon to be the nearer.

However, when size versus brightness was tested, size was found to be the stronger depth cue.

1

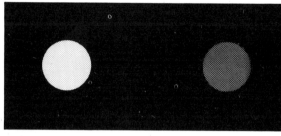

2

3

An experiment conducted by J. J. Gibson compared the cues of size and overlap. For his test, Gibson cut away the corners of two sets of the nearer cards precisely where they "overlapped" the view of the farther cards when seen with one eye from a fixed position through a peephole in his apparatus. This is the view as seen by his subjects.

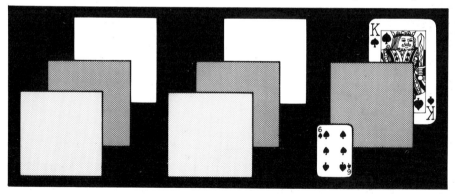

4

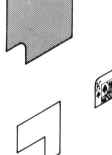

This is the card setup inside the viewing apparatus; in fact, the top right-hand cards in the center and right groups were nearer to the subjects but were identified as being "behind" those on the bottom left (the playing cards are actually the same size). Gibson found that the overlap cue, even when spatially reversed, was so powerful that it negated all the other secondary depth cues.

5

37

The Rudiments of Perspective: One-Point

Perspective is one of the most important facets of the way in which we perceptually structure our understanding of spatial scale and proportion in graphics. As the camera--albeit mechanically--comes somewhat close to explaining this experience, we continue our sequence of image undressing with a simple exercise that aims to locate perspective coordinates in photographs.

1

3

However, once the vanishing point has been located, a horizontal line drawn through it on the face of the photograph establishes the eye level, or horizon line, i.e., the line corresponding to the observer's eye level or, as in this case, the height of the camera lens above ground level.

2 For instance, if we were to move the vanishing point to either side, i.e., as if the photographer had used a slightly different camera angle, its new location would cause wall planes to readjust in response to the subtle change in viewpoint direction.

The position of the horizon line--and its attendant vanishing point--above ground level controls our view of all horizontal planes, including the ground plane. For instance, if the camera had been elevated to roof level, the resultant photograph would have presented a bird's-eye view. **4**

First, select a photograph that looks head-on into a rectangular space, such as a street or a corridor. Then rule lines that trace the edges of planes that run parallel to the line of sight expressed by the view. When these lines are extended into the space of the photograph, they will appear to converge on a common point. This is known as the vanishing point, i.e., the point that controls the direction of view.

5 Conversely, if the camera (and our eye level) had been lowered, and the photograph taken with the camera placed on the ground, the resultant picture would have produced a worm's-eye view.

38

The Rudiments of Perspective: Two-Point

1

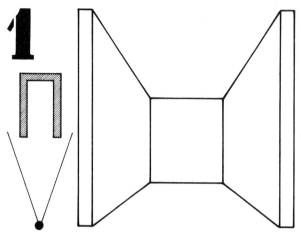

One-point perspective is a means of representing space in which all converging planes are parallel to the onlooker's line of vision. Also, planes that face the viewer remain parallel to the picture plane, i.e., the imaginary plane represented by the drawing surface.

Now let's continue our undressing sequence by retracing the upper and lower edges of the two converging rectangular faces of a cubic form, such as in this photograph of a building. We then project these lines back into the space to either side of its form. **3**

2 By contrast, two-point perspective responds to a shifted viewpoint that sees the planes of an object when not at right angles to the line of vision, such as the "three-quarter" view of a box.

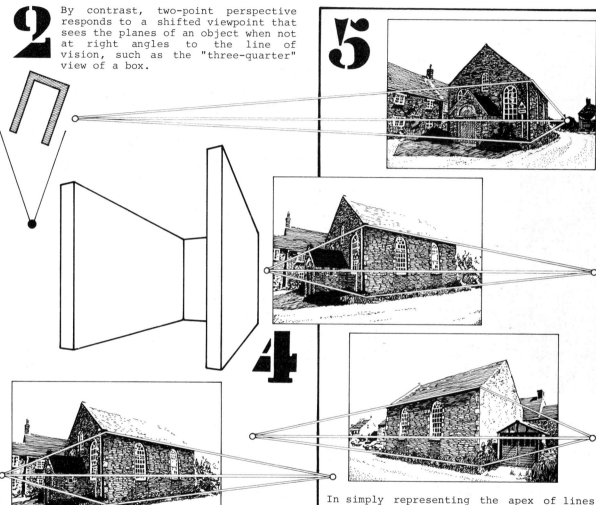

You may find that, unlike one-point perspective, the respective vanishing points may occur outside the picture's format. However, once established, they can be used to locate the horizon line, i.e., the line that represents the height of the view above ground when the building was photographed.

4

In simply representing the apex of lines that describe the angles of converging planes, the respective locations of vanishing points respond directly to the particular viewing angle. For instance, if the photographer had walked around this building to shoot a series of different views, the relative positions of the pairs of vanishing points would have adjusted to each successive view and the corresponding distortion in the angles of converging side planes.

Identifying Message Areas

1

A further factor in our sequence of analyzing graphics is the actual reason for their existence. This is because every kind of image has a message to impart; otherwise, there would be no reason for its existence. The term "message area" refers to that part of the format in which the meaning of an image is conveyed. This special zone is also referred to as the "center of attention," or the "focal point." For example, the message area in this World War One poster is obvious because, in functioning as the focal point, the pointing finger engages the viewer in the center of attention. The graphic attempt to "reach out" and occupy the space between viewer and picture plane is a common device in all kinds of ads. Here, a forced perspective is usually used for the message, or the product, in order to grab attention to it.

2

A good means of understanding the role and location of message areas is to examine all kinds of graphics. For example, in this automobile ad, three aspects of its message area should be noted: its elevated position in the format avoids the predictability of a central location; its sharply focused presence is emphasized by a surrounding and diffused setting (amplified by a color change in the original); and, when rationalized, all the foreground elements--including the text--function as overt and covert directional signals that encourage the eye toward the message area.

3

Apart from the directional signals represented by the gaze of the two onlookers, this automobile ad uses an extreme example of contrast in technique. Here, the use of color photography for the automobile and the nearest figure, superimposed on a black and white setting of a cartoonlike drawing, leaves the viewer in no doubt about the message area and, indeed, the message (see page 127).

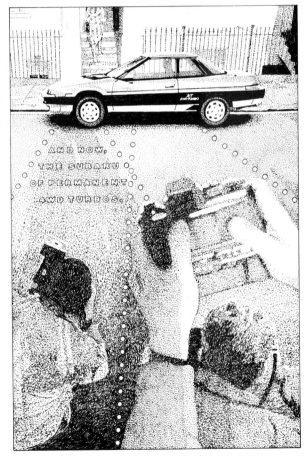

Identifying Message Areas: George Dombek

This drawing is adapted from a large original by the painter George Dombek of a skeletal roof structure of one of Florida's tobacco barns left damaged in the wake of a hurricane. Notice that the center of attention is off-center and that its presence is emphasized by using contrasting levels of information. In this case, a contrast is emphasized between the intensity, scale, and proximity of positive and negative (black and white) patterns.

Identifying Spatial Structure

However, if we redefine a small portion of the panorama, the spatial structure changes drastically. It now presents a more formal view in which what was at first open and free is now strictly enclosed by the presence of defining planes. Developed from a drawing by Feilden Clegg Design.

Each pictorial image that we confront is also governed by its own spatial structure. This structure represents a modification, or interruption, of the continuous flow of the space it describes. Each modification is, in turn, controlled by the number and complexity of planes and edges that exist to shape its particular configuration. For instance, in this panoramic view the format is filled with a seemingly limitless and unimpeded space that apparently flows beyond the confines of its frame.

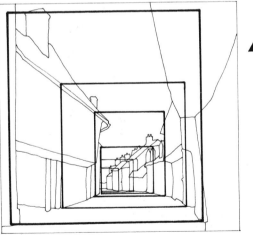

The characteristic of each spatial structure dictates the manner in which it is "read." This drawing utilizes a more enclosed "window" through which the eye is sucked into the more open space beyond.

The degree of openness and closure of space is one means of understanding the composition of graphics. In our process of undressing images we can now analyze them in terms of their spatial organization. For instance, this degree of enclosure represents the graphic funnel.

Funneled space is created from a succession of framed "windows" formed by the edges of side planes that induce the eye to explore a series of spatial events--each being defined by the frame of its predecessor.

42

Identifying Spatial Structure

Filtered views represent a third means of connecting two pockets of graphic space. In this kind of spatial connection, the eye reconstructs fragments of glimpsed information that are seen between foreground and middleground, and middleground and background.

N.B.: The three basic ways of enclosing the spatial continuum, i.e., framing, funneling, and filtering, are commonly found in drawings, paintings, and photographs. Indeed, they are exactly the same means of three-dimensional articulation used by the sculptor, architect, and urban designer. In any case, our technique of dismantling graphics is a method that you should employ to determine the variety of pictorial structures of space across a gamut of different images.

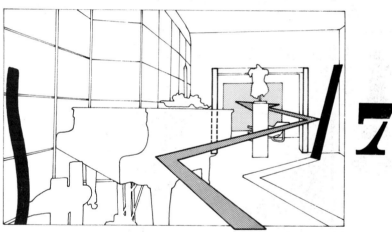

You will discover that more visually interesting compositions result from more sophisticated combinations of spatial features. For instance, this drawing enlists the functions of framing, subframing, and filtering as a means of gradually disclosing its focal point to the eye as it journeys along an indirect route to the message area.

In his book _Graphic Communication as a Design Tool_, Omar Faruque suggests that the skill involved in creating visually compelling spatial structures relies upon the availability of features to frame and fashion space without disrupting the sense of continuity. However, the key to a successful compositional structure is the careful selection of viewpoint. Therefore, when studying graphics you should be aware of your viewing position as dictated by the nature of each type of spatial enclosure.

The Invisible Dynamics of Graphics

1

If we now extend these traced analytical lines so that they connect with other lines and also cut across the picture plane, the structural character and two-dimensional balance of an image are exposed.

2

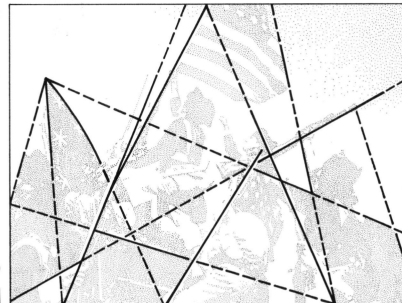

3

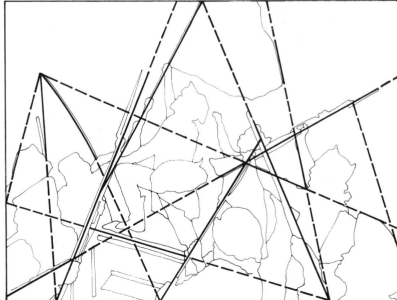

A traditional means of analyzing the essence of a graphic is to expose its underlying construction lines. This is done by tracing the edges of the main objects in the composition to expose a network of horizontal, vertical, and diagonal lines. Any comparative analysis between various images will reveal quite different pictorial structures, which, in turn, reflect different two-dimensional movements.

It is now only a short step to identifying the underlying geometric pattern that, although not always obvious in the original, controls the character of the image. It was the recognition of such non-objective structures that possibly marked the point of departure for abstract painting at the turn of the century.

44

The Invisible Dynamics of Graphics

4

We can now examine an image in terms of the invisible tensions that are generated by its spatial structure. To do this we must first reduce a picture to its fundamental outlines, i.e., delineate its compartments of solid and negative volume into a flat abstract pattern of shape.

5

The main formal volumes comprising the picture should now be further reduced into their respective networks of faceted planes.

A tension is seen to occur between the planes, especially at their points of overlap-- the greater the apparent space between, the greater the tension.

If we now insert the long and short axes into these planes, we diagram their individual directional movement and indicate their static and dynamic relationship to each other and to the picture plane.

6

7

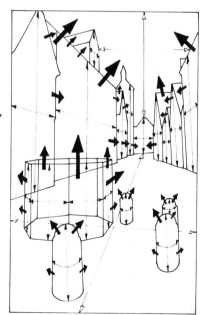

8

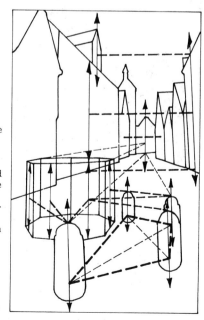

Another form of tension is created by the interplay of planes across the negative space confined by the picture plane. This complex structure of tension occurs in all pictorial systems, and functions to indicate the amount and extent of implied space.

The Invisible Dynamics of Graphics

Yet another form of tension is seen to be generated by the relationship between the axes of dominant planes in a composition. We can begin to understand this kind of tension in this analysis of a computer-generated graphic. This recognition and visual linking of the major but invisible pictorial forces are similar to the way we tend to perceptually group like objects.

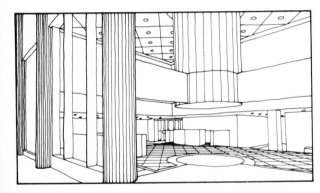

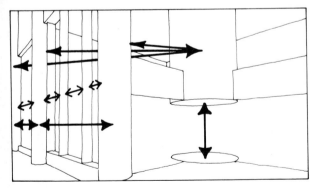

This analysis of a photograph illustrates a common form of spatial composition in graphics. It shows a revolving movement around an off-center axis. While the illusion of space is enhanced by the tensions caused by overlapping forms around the central focal point, the eye is brought into the picture and induced to follow a circular path that takes it on a trip from the left foreground to the middleground, where the location of the main axis coincides with the message area. The eye is then returned from the depth of the illusion, via a continuation of the circular path, to complete its route in the right foreground. This compositional ability, which allows the eye to enter, move through, and exit the spatial arrangement of a graphic, is emphasized in William Kirby Lockard's book <u>Design Drawing</u>. He uses the analogy of a bouncing ball to demonstrate the movement of the spectator's eye into and out of the space of a drawing.

This method of analysis and those on pages 43-44 are based on studies of Cézanne's paintings made by Erle Loran.

3 MEDIUMS, MARKS, AND SKETCHES

Pencils

1 The pencil represents the cheapest, most versatile and easily accessible form of drawing instrument. Pencils come in many forms but, generally, can be subdivided into three basic types.

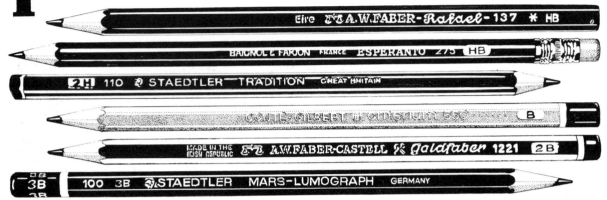

Traditional wood-encased pencils contain a core of graphite that is available in a range of softness and hardness--usually the softer the grade, the thicker the "lead" core.

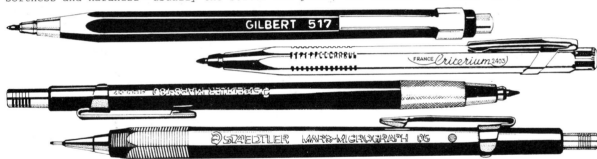

Mechanical, or clutch, pencils employ a push-button action on their plastic and/or metal barrels; this feeds leads made from high polymer or graphite that are available in a full range of hardness, thickness, and color.

The "heavyweight" specialist pencils, such as ebony and carbon pencils and the oval-shaped carpenter's pencil with its oval-shaped lead, contain thick, soft black leads ideal for making large sketches. Their crayonlike boldness relates more to freedom of expression than to precision work.

The versatility of the pencil results from its interaction with the degree of textural grain presented by the drawing surface, the degree of finger-applied pressure during its movement about the paper, and the grade of graphite used. Graphite grades range in descending scales of hardness from 9H to F, and in ascending scales of softness from HB to EE. Generally speaking, pencils represented by the H scale are more suited to technical drafting and will indent softer papers if subjected to extreme pressure. Conversely, pencils represented by the B scale are more conducive to freehand drawing and sketching, with HB and B being ideal for general drawing.

9H
8H
7H
6H
5H
4H
3H
2H
H
F
HB
B
2B
3B
4B
5B
6B
EB
EE

2

Pencil Pointers

The versatility of the pencil allows lines to be drawn in any direction and at different pressures, or "weights," and at different drawing angles. Therefore, the pencil functions as an ideal drawing instrument for a wide spectrum of drawings --from the lightning sketch to the most meticulous of observations. Since there is hardly a drawing that will not require some straight lines, practice drawing them freehand and with one purposeful motion.

N.B.: As a general rule, avoid combining the hard and the soft graphite grades in one drawing.

1 Good pencil technique relies upon a proper pencil-point maintenance. A good, regular drawing point should be hand-sharpened (rather than mechanically sharpened) to achieve enough exposure of the graphite core for pointing without reducing the effective support of its wood case.

3 A chisel point is achieved by shaping the end of the graphite rod on a sanding block while holding the pencil at the normal drawing angle. The chisel point has the potential of producing both broad-stroke lines and--when the point is inverted to present its sharp edge--beautifully fine lines.

4 Erasing should be viewed as a means of inserting highlights into a drawing rather than as a means of removing errors. The best eraser is the pliable "kneaded" version that can be either shaped as a ball for pressing down onto a pencil tone and plucked away to leave a lightened area, or . . .

5 . . . pinched into a point for "cutting" light accents into a pencil tone.

N.B.: Generally, avoid erasure by rubbing, as this will tend to smear graphite and degrade the freshness and receptivity of the drawing paper.

Introducing the Pencil to the Hand

The common drawing grasp holds the pencil between 1" (25mm) and 2" (50mm) from the lead. This affords maximum control over its movement about the paper.

2 Varying angles of pencil address to the paper are used for different thicknesses and qualities of line. For example, the more acute the angle, the thicker and less precise the line.

Usually, the nearer the fingers to the lead, the more the control. However, you should try holding the pencil at different distances from the lead, remembering that the pencil should feel comfortable in the hand with the fingers relaxed.

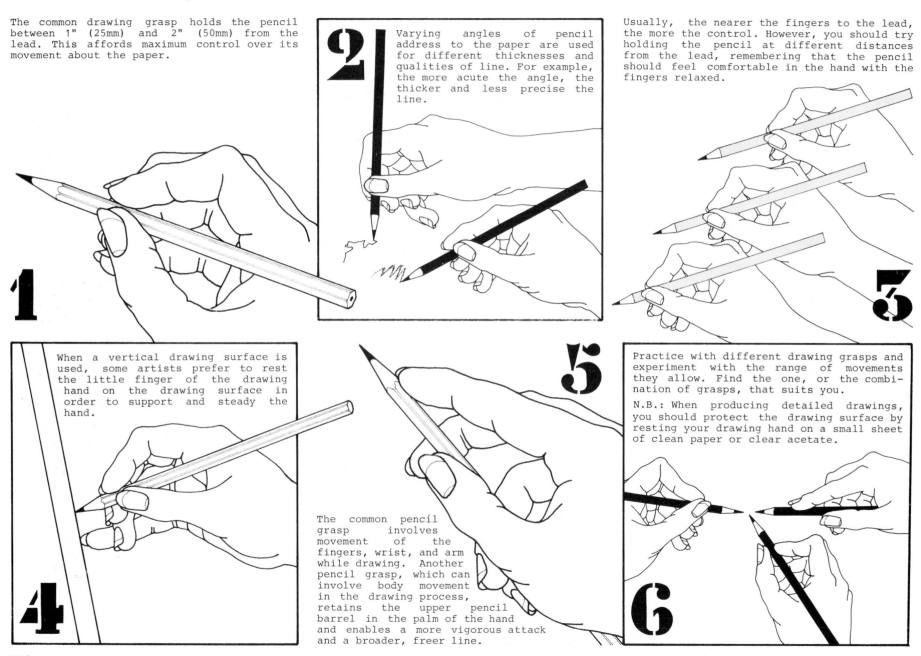

4 When a vertical drawing surface is used, some artists prefer to rest the little finger of the drawing hand on the drawing surface in order to support and steady the hand.

The common pencil grasp involves movement of the fingers, wrist, and arm while drawing. Another pencil grasp, which can involve body movement in the drawing process, retains the upper pencil barrel in the palm of the hand and enables a more vigorous attack and a broader, freer line.

Practice with different drawing grasps and experiment with the range of movements they allow. Find the one, or the combination of grasps, that suits you.

N.B.: When producing detailed drawings, you should protect the drawing surface by resting your drawing hand on a small sheet of clean paper or clear acetate.

Introducing the Pencil to Paper

1 It is important to experience the effect of the various grades of graphite on a range of different drawing-paper surfaces because such an experience will enhance the ability to match the appropriate pencil to the selected drawing surface. Every type of drawing paper has a surface grain, or tooth, that --in the action of drawing--scrapes the graphite from the pencil and holds it intact. The rougher the tooth, the more graphite will be retained by the surface; the softer the lead, the more graphite will be deposited on the surface. Begin by laying down an even graphite wash on a smooth-surfaced bristol board (cartridge paper) using a 4B grade pencil . . .

. . . and then a 2H grade pencil. Notice the difference in quality between the heavier weight of value offered by the softer graphite and the lighter, almost metallic, silver quality offered by the harder graphite.

2 Next, try a whole range of graphite grades in the production of values on four different drawing-paper surfaces. Explore the differences between the grades of graphite in the creation of even-toned and graduated washes, and in the spontaneity of an unrestricted application of value.

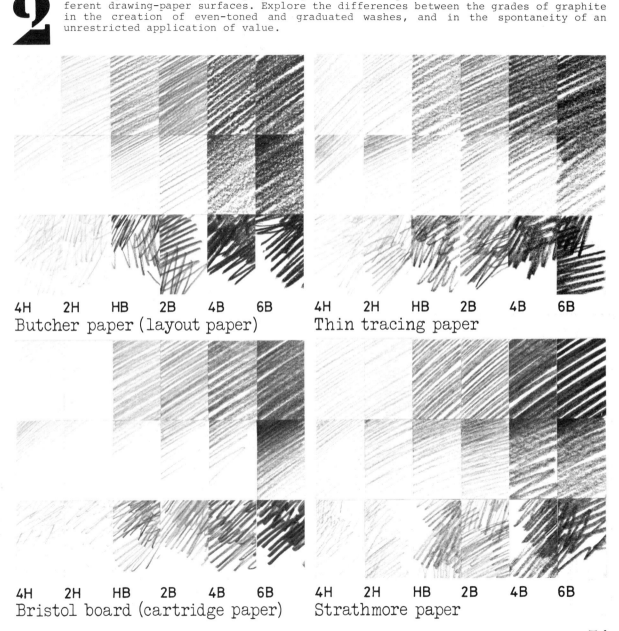

4H   2H   HB   2B   4B   6B
Butcher paper (layout paper)

4H   2H   HB   2B   4B   6B
Thin tracing paper

4H   2H   HB   2B   4B   6B
Bristol board (cartridge paper)

4H   2H   HB   2B   4B   6B
Strathmore paper

Pencil Line: Contour Drawing

This drawing exercise requires a 6B pencil, drawing board, and paper, and total concentration.

Sitting close to the subject for the drawing, focus your eye on a pre-selected starting point along the outer edge of the object in view. Then, after placing the pencil point on the drawing paper, imagine that it is actually touching the object at the very point that is the subject of your gaze. This concept may take time to achieve conviction. Therefore, remain studying the subject until you are convinced that your pencil is aimed at the focal point of your vision. Once this concept has gained credibility, the drawing can begin.

N.B.: The techniques of contour and gesture drawing described here and on the facing page derive from the teachings of the late Kimon Nicolaides. They are recorded in his posthumous work <u>The Natural Way to Draw</u>.

1

Now move your eye slowly along the contour of the object while simultaneously moving your pencil along the paper. As your pencil responds to the eye's tracking of the contour, you should maintain the conviction that the pencil point is actually touching the contour.

The fact that you are being guided by the sense of touch rather than sight means that you must draw without looking at the paper. By continuously looking at the object, you are developing a coordination of pencil and eye.

2

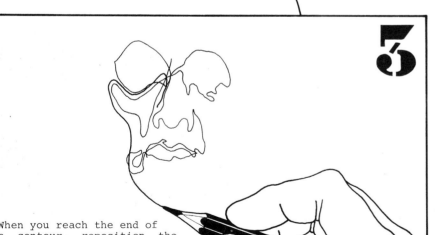

3

When you reach the end of a contour, reposition the pencil on the paper and, before proceeding, mentally reaffirm your conviction of touch by studying a second contour. Continue this process until the contours are exhausted.

Three types of contours may be encountered: those that trace the outer edge of the object; those that trace the negative space of shapes within the object; and those that are formed from overlapping, projected elements. Each contour type is determined as you glance down to reposition the pencil before resuming your fixation on the object.

4

Pencil Line: Gesture Drawing

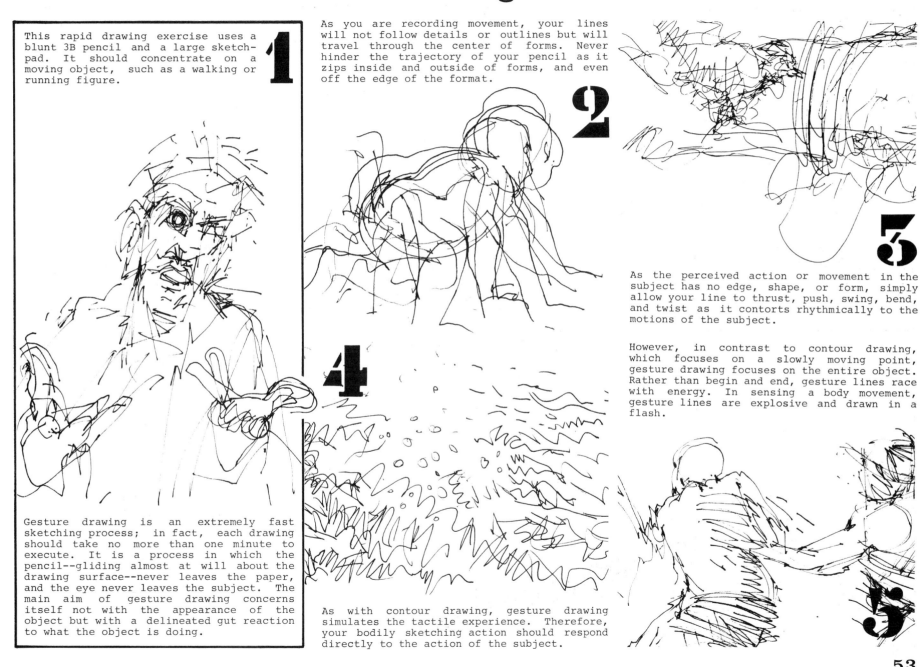

This rapid drawing exercise uses a blunt 3B pencil and a large sketchpad. It should concentrate on a moving object, such as a walking or running figure.

Gesture drawing is an extremely fast sketching process; in fact, each drawing should take no more than one minute to execute. It is a process in which the pencil--gliding almost at will about the drawing surface--never leaves the paper, and the eye never leaves the subject. The main aim of gesture drawing concerns itself not with the appearance of the object but with a delineated gut reaction to what the object is doing.

As you are recording movement, your lines will not follow details or outlines but will travel through the center of forms. Never hinder the trajectory of your pencil as it zips inside and outside of forms, and even off the edge of the format.

As with contour drawing, gesture drawing simulates the tactile experience. Therefore, your bodily sketching action should respond directly to the action of the subject.

As the perceived action or movement in the subject has no edge, shape, or form, simply allow your line to thrust, push, swing, bend, and twist as it contorts rhythmically to the motions of the subject.

However, in contrast to contour drawing, which focuses on a slowly moving point, gesture drawing focuses on the entire object. Rather than begin and end, gesture lines race with energy. In sensing a body movement, gesture lines are explosive and drawn in a flash.

Pens

1 The pen is the oldest drawing instrument, its forerunner possibly being a stick dipped in pigment. Modern pens dispense their ink in two ways: either from a built-in reservoir or via a constant refueling by dipping into an ink source. Nib characteristics and their attendant mark-making abilities vary dramatically both within and across the four basic families of pens.

Fountain pens make an ideal sketching medium--their flexible nibs already being responsive to hand and finger movements. Furthermore, as sketching can be considered an extension of handwriting, their familiarity and portability make them an excellent medium for the beginner.

By contrast, dip pens require some experience in their use. This group of drawing pens includes a vast range of nib types, from the traditional school steel pen and the mapping pen to the traditional reed, cane, or quill pen, together with a host of pens with interchangeable specialist drawing nibs, such as the Gillott and the Hunt ranges.

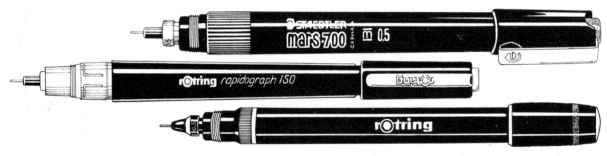

Technical pens are designed to produce even, continuous lines in a range of thicknesses offered by their interchangeable tubular steel nibs. This makes them more suited to technical drafting than to freehand sketching and the ease of line expression associated with it.

Ballpoint pens have enjoyed recent advances in their development. Newly evolved versions, such as the Uni-ball, can simulate the precision of fine-line technical pens, while others, such as the Ball Pentel and Pentel Superball, permit a widely expressive line quality never before achievable with this medium.

54

2

As the characteristic of each type of nib has a tremendous influence on the nature of the resultant drawing, it is important to put each pen through its paces on a smooth drawing paper. Practice various line movements, pressures, and speeds; discover how different pens behave, such as the versatility of the steel-nib pen, the scratchy line of the mapping pen, the controlled line of the technical pen, and the sheer speed and pizzazz of the ballpoint pen. When selecting a dip pen holder, avoid the thinner types in favor of one that has the same weight and thickness as your fountain pen.

Introducing the Pen

As with all drawing instruments, the pen should be held with a relaxed hand--the little finger resting lightly on the drawing surface for support. When dip pens are used, the action for drawing short lines, such as in the construction of hatches and the recording of fine detail, is much like that of a fountain pen, i.e., a finger-induced action in which increased pressure produces thicker line weights.

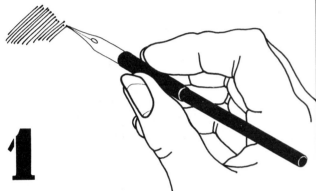

1

2

Longer pen flourishes incorporate finger and wrist movements, while the supporting little finger steadies the line-making operation as the hand glides over the paper.

3

The finer the nib, the smoother the paper will have to be in order to allow the point to glide about the drawing surface. Bristol board is best for the delicate lines of steel nibs, while the tooth of Strathmore paper offers more resistance.

4

Watercolor paper--although not commonly used for ink drawing --induces a rough-paper technique. However, the more heavily textured papers should be reserved only for the characteristic effects that they encourage.

5

There are two basic types of drawing ink: waterproof and soluble. Specially formulated waterproof ink is ideal for technical pens, while only soluble "permanent" ink should be employed in fountain pens to avoid corroding their insides. Both waterproof and soluble inks are used with dip pens and can be diluted with purified water--preferably boiled or distilled--or rainwater.

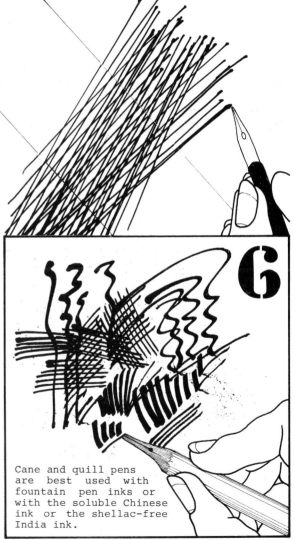

6

Cane and quill pens are best used with fountain pen inks or with the soluble Chinese ink or the shellac-free India ink.

Basic Pen Lines, Values, and Textures

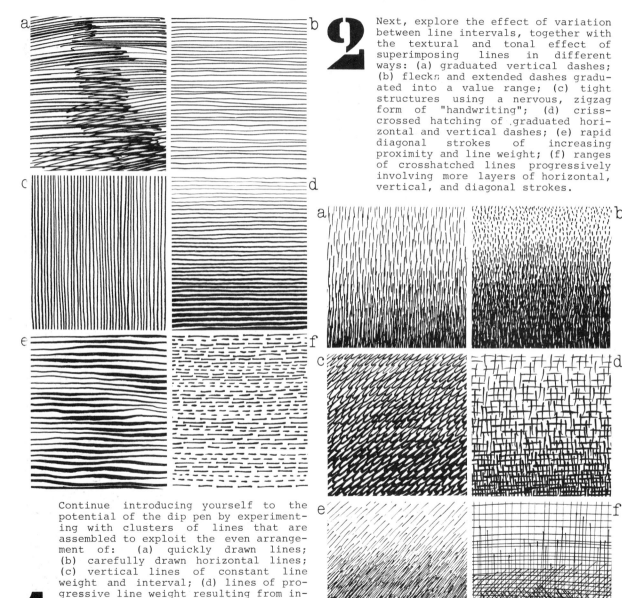

2 Next, explore the effect of variation between line intervals, together with the textural and tonal effect of superimposing lines in different ways: (a) graduated vertical dashes; (b) flecks and extended dashes graduated into a value range; (c) tight structures using a nervous, zigzag form of "handwriting"; (d) crisscrossed hatching of graduated horizontal and vertical dashes; (e) rapid diagonal strokes of increasing proximity and line weight; (f) ranges of crosshatched lines progressively involving more layers of horizontal, vertical, and diagonal strokes.

1 Continue introducing yourself to the potential of the dip pen by experimenting with clusters of lines that are assembled to exploit the even arrangement of: (a) quickly drawn lines; (b) carefully drawn horizontal lines; (c) vertical lines of constant line weight and interval; (d) lines of progressive line weight resulting from increasing pressure on the nib; (e) individual lines expressing variation of pressure along their length; (f) broken lines formed from dots and dashes.

3 As your experience develops, create extended progressions of line-constructed values that, in necessitating a control of both increasing line weight and decreasing proximity, aim to simulate an even gradation from light to dark, such as: (a) using short vertical strokes that increase in weight and proximity; (b) using a controlled and meandering "scribble" of increasing line thickness and complexity; (c) using a loose crosshatched line structure that exploits increasingly multi-directional lines.

N.B.: Aim for a smooth transition between the extremities of each value scale, i.e., avoid a "stepped" appearance.

Basic Ruled Pen Lines and Values

1 As pen lines are more conducive to reproduction, it is important to master as wide a range of their marks as possible. Therefore, with the addition of a ruler, a whole new series of mark-making possibilities opens up to the designer.

N.B.: To avoid the ink bleeding by contact with the straightedge, it is vital that a beveled-edge ruler is used.

2 Begin by dipping your pen in ink and confidently ruling a series of regularly spaced lines of even line weight. Aim to keep each line about 1/16" (1.5mm) away from its neighbors.

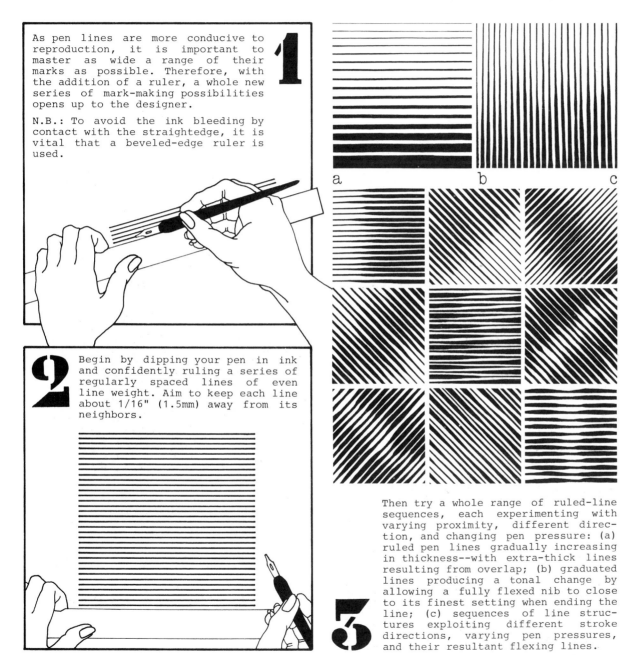

Then try a whole range of ruled-line sequences, each experimenting with varying proximity, different direction, and changing pen pressure: (a) ruled pen lines gradually increasing in thickness--with extra-thick lines resulting from overlap; (b) graduated lines producing a tonal change by allowing a fully flexed nib to close to its finest setting when ending the line; (c) sequences of line structures exploiting different stroke directions, varying pen pressures, and their resultant flexing lines.

3

4 Finally, (a) experience the optical effects of a controlled variation in line and interval width in the ruled construction of the illusion of a corrugated plane, and (b) attempt a complete value scale using mechanical cross-hatching. The latter begins with an all-over "wash" of evenly spaced vertical lines and, via a sequence of graduated steps, descends the value scale by the progressive introduction of all-over horizontal lines followed by two layers of 45-degree lines, first from one direction and, then, from the other.

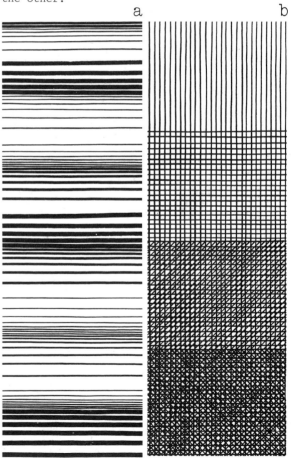

How to Make a Bamboo Cane Pen

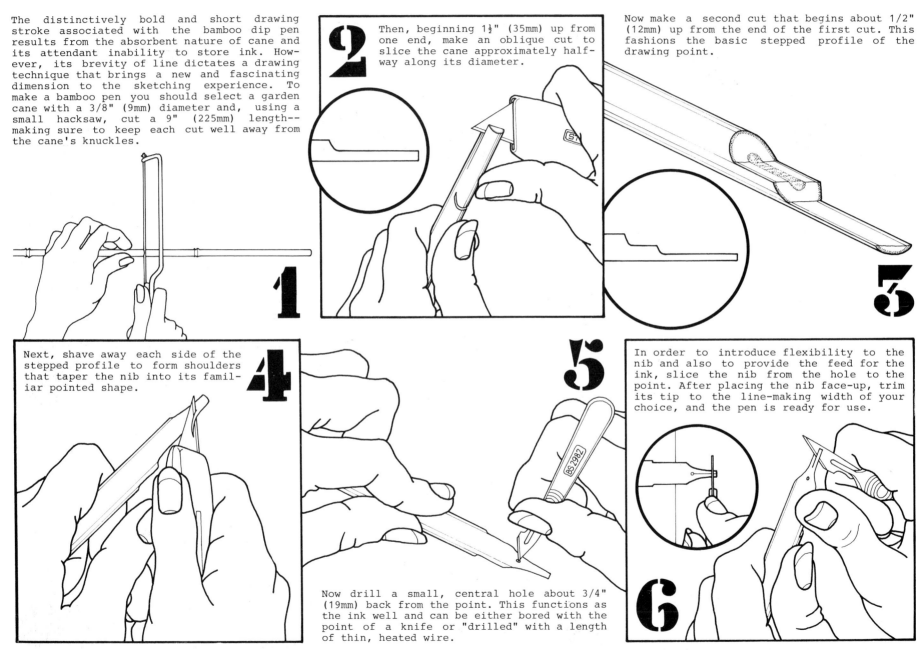

The distinctively bold and short drawing stroke associated with the bamboo dip pen results from the absorbent nature of cane and its attendant inability to store ink. However, its brevity of line dictates a drawing technique that brings a new and fascinating dimension to the sketching experience. To make a bamboo pen you should select a garden cane with a 3/8" (9mm) diameter and, using a small hacksaw, cut a 9" (225mm) length--making sure to keep each cut well away from the cane's knuckles.

1

Then, beginning 1½" (35mm) up from one end, make an oblique cut to slice the cane approximately half-way along its diameter.

2

Now make a second cut that begins about 1/2" (12mm) up from the end of the first cut. This fashions the basic stepped profile of the drawing point.

3

Next, shave away each side of the stepped profile to form shoulders that taper the nib into its familiar pointed shape.

4

Now drill a small, central hole about 3/4" (19mm) back from the point. This functions as the ink well and can be either bored with the point of a knife or "drilled" with a length of thin, heated wire.

5

In order to introduce flexibility to the nib and also to provide the feed for the ink, slice the nib from the hole to the point. After placing the nib face-up, trim its tip to the line-making width of your choice, and the pen is ready for use.

6

How to Make a Quill Pen

1

The quill pen represents the earliest form of dip pen. It is also the most versatile. This is because it is sensitive to the touch and allows a smooth drawing action with none of the scratching associated with steel nibs. To make a quill pen you need first to acquire a large turkey or goose feather. After carefully removing all its barbs and filaments, trim the shaft to a length of 8" (200mm).

2 Using an extremely sharp blade, now make a sloping cut starting about 1" (25mm) from the thicker end of the quill shaft.

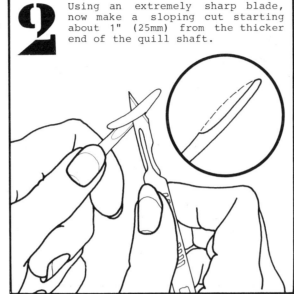

Follow this with a second, more oblique, cut which begins about 1/4" (6mm) from the end of the quill. This second cut forms the basic stepped profile of the nib.

3

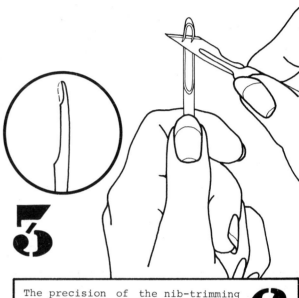

4 Next, slice the nib centrally about 1/4" (6mm) up from the tip of its newly formed point.

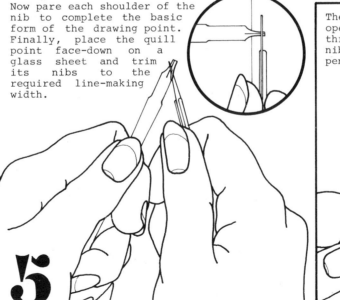

Now pare each shoulder of the nib to complete the basic form of the drawing point. Finally, place the quill point face-down on a glass sheet and trim its nibs to the required line-making width.

5

The precision of the nib-trimming operation should be checked through a magnifying glass. If the nibs are aligned, then the quill pen is ready for use. **6**

Pen Sketching

The best way to begin sketching is to capitalize on your familiarity with your fountain pen. Beginners should evolve a sketch via three stages. The first seeks out mass, edge, and shape, which is mapped in line to organize a basic proportional "geometry."

The third stage is extremely important, as it elaborates the under-drawing into values of tone. Their insertion should respond to two observations: the effect of light in creating shade and shadow; the effect of surface and its textural quality. You will discover that these two tonal aspects can be recorded as a single pattern of value--darkest values appearing as nearest the viewer. This third stage also molds the sketch into a unified whole and, simultaneously, increases the illusion of depth.

With some practice, all three stages will gradually blend into one simultaneous sketching technique. This developed experience should also be accompanied by an investigation of different pens so that a sketching vocabulary keeps pace with your developing insight. Initially, you should aim to extract as much as possible from what you observe. However, as this exhaustive seeing process matures and becomes more selective, you should try sketching in line only.

Stage two extends the preliminary linework into the focus of increasing degrees of detailed information--with a clearer level of detail nearer the viewer. As the sketch takes shape, use this phase to check and adjust relationships between the drawn parts.

Pen Sketching: Thor Mann

This series of drawings is from the sketchbooks of Thor Mann, who, using a broad-nibbed Graphos technical pen, produced an illustrated record of his European travels. These drawings--each taking approximately one minute to produce--demonstrate a keen observation in which the descriptive quality of a minimal delineation captures a wealth of information. In striking at the graphic essence of each observation, these drawings also demonstrate the skill of selectivity--a skill that is developed only as a result of a concentrated and continuous experience of the act of sketching (see page 66).

Thor's sketches usually begin with a horizontal or vertical line. In identifying the center of a major mass or the horizon, this guideline immediately challenges the blankness of the paper and establishes the placement of the ensuing delineation.

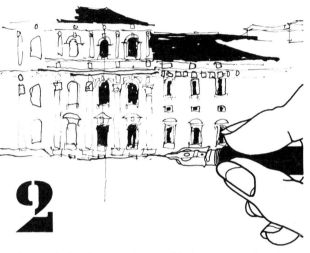

In sketching, the limited mark-making characteristics of the Graphos pen are fully exploited. Its nonflexing nib normally provides a medium stroke; side movements with its edge provide a fine, sinuous line. A broad-stroke effect--useful in simulating shadows and textures--is also achieved by addressing the paper at an acute angle while dragging the side of the nib across the drawing surface.

The Pen-and-Wash Technique

Combining pen lines with brush-applied ranges of gray value washes is an effective sketching technique. This usually begins with the basic ink line drawing.

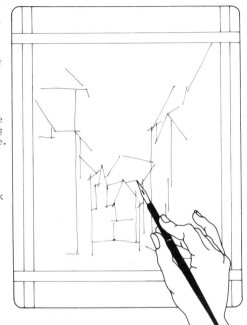

1

The ink drawing should be made with a pen that you feel comfortable with, using a waterproof ink so that the drawing won't dissolve under ensuing washes.

N.B.: If you feel intimidated by either the blankness of the paper or the permanence of the ink, preplan the drawing in light pencil.

2

If a pencil under-drawing has been used, the graphite image can be directly traced in ink or be used as a guide for development into more intricate levels of detail. When penwork is finished and dry, remove the pencil under-drawing with a soft eraser.

3

As you work progressively from light to dark, you can introduce various dilutions of the drawing ink into the composition with a No. 6 brush.

N.B.: If required, excess amounts of wash can be removed, or lightened, by dabbing with a blotter.

4

If soft-edged washes are required, first dampen the required areas with a wash of clean water. This allows the ensuing wash to spread and bleed. Areas of the drawing should not be predampened where a sharp-edged wash is required.

5

6

Aim to utilize areas of white paper to simulate the lightest values, and also to extend your value range. When the wash application is finished and dry, final adjustments to the line drawing can be made with the pen.

Felt- and Fiber-Tipped Markers

Since their advent in the 1950s, markers have been considered as inferior to the pencil and the pen but, in the current age of rapid visualization, they have now come of age. Indeed, markers offer a freshness of line, together with an immediate and brilliant spectrum of value and color, and are also capable of producing marks comparable to those achieved by the pen and the brush. Generally, markers dispense two types of ink: permanent spirit-based ink and water-soluble ink. Their extensive range of mark-making abilities falls into three main categories: wide-, medium-, and fine-tipped.

1

The range of line potential produced by markers stems from their extensive range of nib types. These include the wide- and soft-tipped felt tips in round, square, oblique, and chisel shapes, through the conical semisoft bullet tips, and on to the fine-line and ultra-fine-line tips of the composition, nylon, and fiber-tipped markers.

2

Marker values range from those that are laid down as broad-stroke "washes," through those line-constructed from a loose spontaneity of the intermediate nib thicknesses, and down to the precision and order achievable by fine-line hatching.

3

WIDE-TIPPED

MEDIUM-TIPPED

FINE-TIPPED

Marker Mark Potential

Drawing paper has to be selected with care, as the spirit-based markers tend to bleed on soft-surfaced and thin papers. Therefore, experiment on a variety of papers, from the harder-surfaced Strathmore and the custom wax-backed marker paper to the texture-surfaced watercolor papers.

1

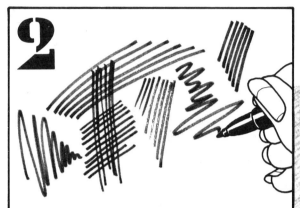

2

Contrary to popular belief, markers can achieve a variety of line qualities. Before sketching, you should experiment with marks made from a variety of pressures and angles of address.

N.B.: Under prolonged periods of pressure the softer felt-tipped nibs tend to wear down and deform.

Markers are expensive and have a limited life. Therefore, always replace the cap, as they quickly dry out when not in use. However, a semidry, black pen can be extremely useful in creating "halftone" textured values.

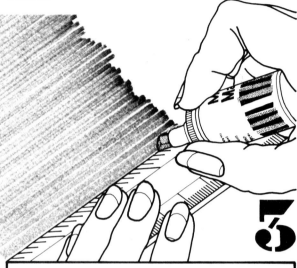

3

The water-based markers do not bleed, but softer effects can be achieved by working on a slightly dampened paper, or be overworked with brush and clean water or watercolor to produce transparent and diffused effects.

4

However, the characteristic bleeding of markers can be used to good effect--especially in more atmospheric graphics. Indeed, some illustrators work a spirit-based marker on the back of thin paper before reversing the sheet to introduce a fine-line drawing into the resultant and diffused effect.

6

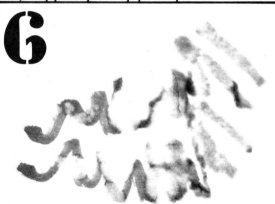

5

Another bleeding technique is to pour droplets of marker solvent, such as Flo-master fluid, onto preselected areas of a drawing. As the fluid spreads it causes a mistlike quality--the extent of which is arrested by application of a blotter.

Marker Sketch-Building Techniques

There are two approaches to sketching in line and value with markers. Both involve the use of three markers: a wide-tipped light gray, a wide-tipped medium gray, and a fine-line black. One approach begins by blocking in the main background, middleground, and foreground value shapes with the light gray marker.

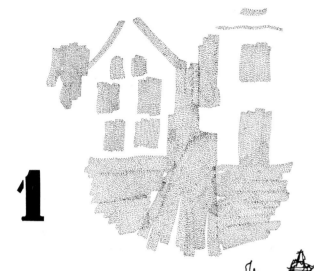

1

3 Finally, shape delineation and value and texture details are overworked using the fine-line black marker. This final stage superimposes a network of detail that acts to structure the sketch into an illusion of three dimensions.

2 The second stage extends the established light gray value pattern with an overlay of middleground and foreground shade and shadow using the medium gray marker.

Conversely, a more conventional approach begins with a fine-line black drawing that seeks to establish all the main shapes and details of the composition.

4

This delineation is then elaborated with progressive layers of the two values of gray: light gray to impart an atmospheric distance; dark gray to denote shade and shadows and a feeling of closeness.

5

Rapid One-Minute Marker Sketches

A good introduction to the quick-fire marker sketching technique is to make a whole series of very fast drawings along a preselected urban route. To do this you need a small sketchbook with a firm cover, a medium-tipped black marker, and a wristwatch or stopwatch.

First, position yourself at the starting point of your route and, facing into the direction of the view, cradle the sketchbook with your lower arm, wearing your wristwatch on your drawing arm for easy reference. You are now going to make a drawing in one minute only. Impossible though this sounds, the time limit should be strictly adhered to, as the main aim of this experience is to coordinate the seeing and drawing functions into one synchronized act. As the experience develops, aim to spend more time looking at the space ahead and--throughout the act of sketching--less time looking at the drawing, i.e., consider the sketch as irrelevant, merely a byproduct of the observation process.

Now, working extremely quickly, make the first sketch of what you see. As drawing time is short, the functions of composing, rescaling, and recording will have to take care of themselves. Simply attack the paper with what you see!

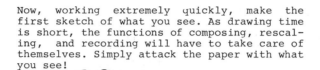

When the minute is up, stop drawing immediately and walk on into the space represented by your first sketch. When the space changes and a new view is seen, stop and make a second one-minute drawing. Continue this procedure throughout your route.

As you continue making rapid sketches along the route, one important fact will emerge, i.e., that you have to make instant decisions about what is important and what is unimportant in each sketch. Superficial marks waste seconds, with the pressure of time forcing you to the graphic essence of each observation.

A morning spent on this exercise can produce around one hundred sketches, each representing a raw gut response to the visual events along the route. Finally, compare initial sketches with those made at the end of the session. You will find that your facility for observation and recording has improved drastically.

Charcoal and Crayons

Charcoal is made from charred willow or ash and is supplied in various thicknesses and forms --natural vine, compressed stick, and wood-encased--each available in soft, medium, and hard grades. There is also a white charcoal pencil for working on dark-toned paper that is also used for introducing highlights into black charcoal renderings. A black powdered version of charcoal is also marketed. When used, albeit rarely, this is applied with a soft cloth for blending large areas of value.

Conté crayon is a form of refined charcoal stick, as it is harder, finer, less dusty, but slightly more greasy. Made in France, it is imported in a limited range of colors including black, white, sepia, and sanguine. It is made in both stick and pencil form and is ideal for sketching.

Blackboard chalk is brittle and gritty. It is produced in assorted colors and can be mixed with charcoal or Conté crayon for creating highlight effects.

Black wax crayons and China markers, or "grease" pencils, produce dense, glossy lines that work on almost any kind of surface. Being water-repellent, they can be used as a resist under ink and colored pencil washes. Wax crayons can be sharpened with a blade for producing finer lines, while many China markers are available in the self-sharpening form, i.e., by unwinding the case to expose a new length of wax rod.

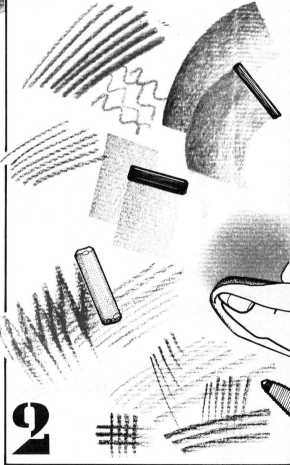

Explore all the possibilities of charcoal and crayons. The virtues of these mediums --in the unencased state--are not necessarily confined to their points. By using the entire length flat on the paper, charcoal, Conté crayon, and school chalk can produce broad, vigorous passages. The corners on the sides of square sticks can also be used effectively for creating sharp, straight, or twisting lines, the quality of which--like all the other marks made by these mediums--can be multiplied indefinitely by using different kinds of paper.

Introducing Charcoal to Paper

1

When used in its natural vine form, charcoal is a gloriously dirty medium and the user has to be prepared for dirty hands. For this reason, the drawing hand should not touch the paper surface during drawing, the resultant freedom of address allowing the arm and body to develop large, sweeping, fluid strokes--the speed of which makes charcoal an ideal medium for rapid sketching.

2

The essential characteristic of charcoal is its sheer boldness, blackness, and wide potential of value on all kinds of paper, from tissue paper, brown paper, and newsprint to the finest-quality boards.

3

Highlights in charcoal drawings can easily be "erased," or blended, using a compressed ball of bread, a kneaded eraser, a cloth, a tortillon (a paper stump of rolled paper), a cotton bud, or, best of all, the fingers.

4

Try making a large drawing on toned or tinted paper, such as brown paper. In producing an overall middle value, the paper provides a base for applying descending steps of dark value using black charcoal, and ascending steps of lighter values using white Conté crayon or chalk.

5

The instability of charcoal (together with that of Conté crayon and chalk) means that finished drawings have to be fixed for their protection against smudging. This can be quickly accomplished using an aerosol fixative or an aerosol hair lacquer.

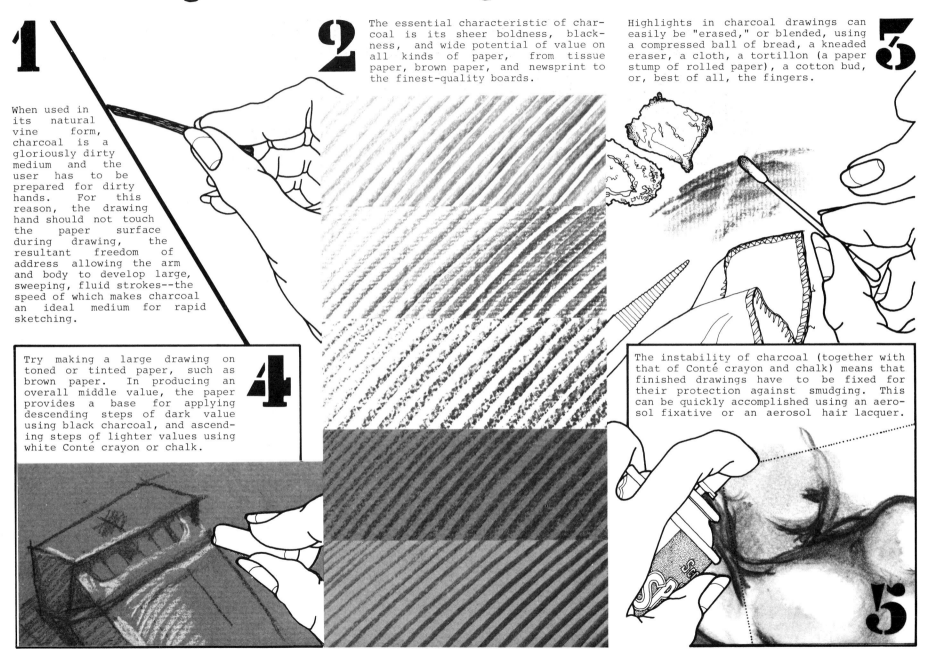

4 FREEHAND DRAWING TECHNIQUES

Foreground, Middleground, and Background

When we make a drawing of objects in space, an important consideration that will affect its compositional structure is the relationships of foreground, middleground, and background. These pictorial zones are best visualized as a stage set.

1

2

For instance, the background acts as a backcloth against which the "performance," or graphic message, is examined. In providing a stop to the image, background information is less distinct than that in other zones.

The middleground represents "center stage." In graphics this is where the main reason for communicating takes place. Objects in this sector usually appear as complete and in some detail.

3

The handling of the area around the frame--especially to the left--is crucial in compositions, as this is where the eye often enters the picture. With experience, we can employ various devices to steer the eye inward to the message zone--using either direct or indirect routes (see page 131). Drawing based on a photograph by George Bray.

Objects or events that occur at the very front of the "stage," i.e., in the foreground, appear as incomplete. They are larger, generally darker, and in sharp detail. Great care must therefore be taken with their positioning. Avoid blocking the middleground or unintentionally disrupting the frame with projecting elements.

70

Distance and Scale

In drawing, the importance of distance between viewer and subject is demonstrated if we examine these three images. First, this closeup view of a building provides a detailed concentration on an object and its shape and surface quality.

However, if we move away, the same building now occupies middleground rather than foreground space. It now becomes an object viewed within the illusion of the space of its setting, thereby allowing more evidence of its foreground and background.

If we move even farther away, the building now becomes one of a series of objects in the landscape. Rather than scrutinize the building as an object, the eye now wanders freely about the space of its setting.

 The physical size of the drawing, together with its level of detail and range of tonal value, is increased as we move toward the building.

During this transformation by distance, other aspects of a drawing will alter. For example, if we were to sketch only the building from the three vantage points, this would affect the levels of detail and value and the actual size of the drawing. This drawing represents a sketch made from a quarter of a mile away and in which detail is minimized and value is summarized.

 It is important to note that--apart from drastic increase in size, and degrees of detail and value--each stage of proximity reflects a quite different drawing technique.

View-Finding Scale and Size

Once the subject and its distance and angle of view have been chosen, the next step before making the drawing involves the selection of the best possible composition. A useful aid for making this selection is the viewfinder. This is a simple device that mechanically cuts down the profusion of information in the visual field--especially that in the region of peripheral vision. By moving the viewfinder around in the line of sight and peering through its window with one eye closed, you can frame, and isolate for study, the best possible format for the drawing.

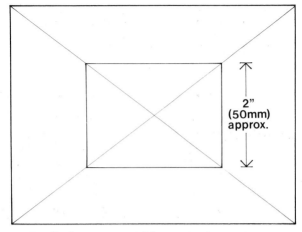

2" (50mm) approx.

A viewfinder is quickly made by cutting a window from a sheet of thin card. This is best made from a sheet that is the same size as your drawing paper. First, draw diagonal lines from each corner of the card before drawing a small rectangle at the center.

2

In working like a camera viewfinder, the card viewfinder can also be used to determine whether the subject should be drawn horizontally, i.e., in a landscape format . . .

4

Once the opening has been cut out, you have produced a window that has a proportion relative to that of your drawing paper. Now, holding the viewfinder in front of your eyes, search for the most interesting composition.

3

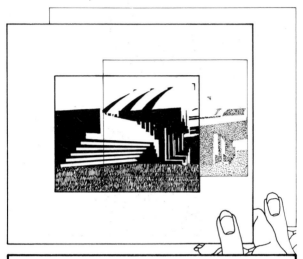

5 . . . or vertically, i.e., in a portrait format.

View-Finding Degrees of Information

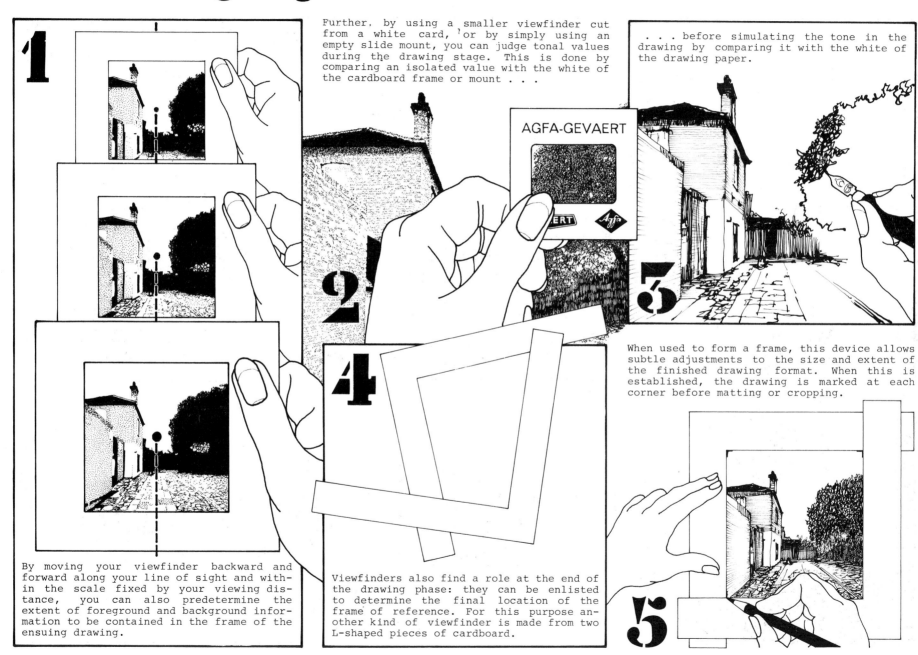

1 By moving your viewfinder backward and forward along your line of sight and within the scale fixed by your viewing distance, you can also predetermine the extent of foreground and background information to be contained in the frame of the ensuing drawing.

2 Further, by using a smaller viewfinder cut from a white card, or by simply using an empty slide mount, you can judge tonal values during the drawing stage. This is done by comparing an isolated value with the white of the cardboard frame or mount . . .

3 . . . before simulating the tone in the drawing by comparing it with the white of the drawing paper.

4 Viewfinders also find a role at the end of the drawing phase: they can be enlisted to determine the final location of the frame of reference. For this purpose another kind of viewfinder is made from two L-shaped pieces of cardboard.

5 When used to form a frame, this device allows subtle adjustments to the size and extent of the finished drawing format. When this is established, the drawing is marked at each corner before matting or cropping.

AGFA-GEVAERT

Measuring with a Pencil

Objective sketching and drawing are a means of training the eye to see and judge scale and proportion. The following is a useful measuring method employed by artists for checking proportion and scale in an evolving drawing. This method utilizes the pencil or other drawing instrument as a measuring device along which the thumb--in acting as a kind of slide rule--is moved to determine the relative widths and heights of elements in the sight size of the field of view before their transfer into the drawing.

First, hold the pencil vertically behind the thumb and present it at arm's length into the field of view. In order for the dimension to be accurately transferred, it is important that all measurements be taken with the arm locked in the out-stretched position and that measurements be sighted with one eye closed.

Align the tip of the pencil with the upper edge of an object prominent in the field of view and slide the thumb into a position so that its tip coincides with the lower edge of the object.

Making sure that this measurement is maintained, transfer the pencil to the drawing surface and make a mental note of the dimension before marking either with the same pencil or with a pencil held in the other hand.

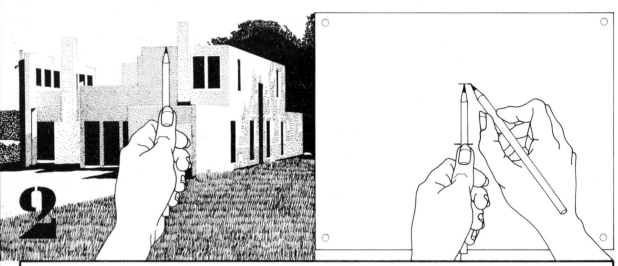

This dimension represents one taken from the sight size in your field of view. Now reassume this measurement against the object in the field of view and, using it as a unit, count the number of units to a second point either above, below, or holding the pencil horizontally, to either side of the original object. This second dimension can be recorded in the drawing.

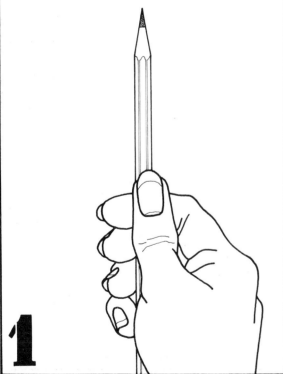

Measuring with a Pencil

This simple process of sighting rescaled dimensions across the format of the visual field can be extended until a basic proportional structure of measurement has been established to guide the next stage of drawing.

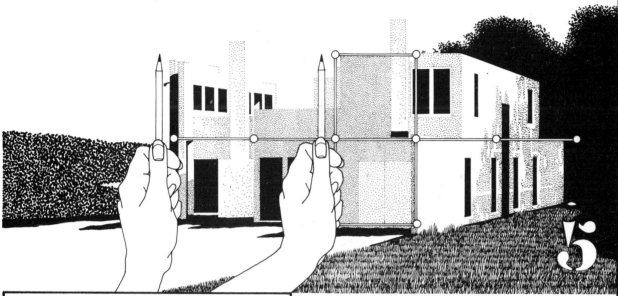

Similarly, when we visually gauge like-sized objects in the depth of space, we can also be fooled by the phenomenon of constancy scaling (see page 26). This measuring technique can be used as a double-check on the widths and heights of objects in the foreground or middleground of our vision relative to those of objects in the background.

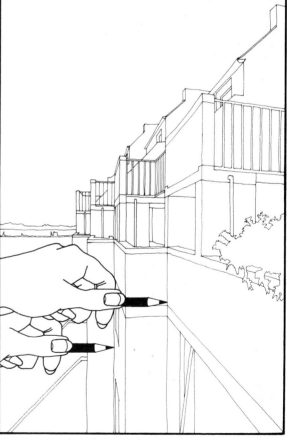

For the beginner, a good introduction to this system of measurement is the comparison of the width and height of a cubic form.

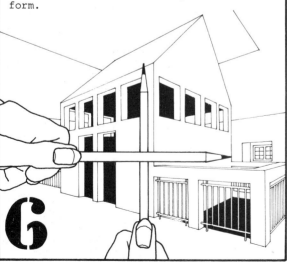

This technique is important to visual accuracy because we can easily be fooled by apparent dimensions in our field of vision. This deception is shown by this illusion of a top hat. Which has the longer dimension: the brim or the crown? Check your mental response using the pencil-thumb measuring method.

Other Measuring Aids: Angles

2 Once determined, the angle can be now established in the drawing by bringing the pencil and its description of the angle to the drawing surface. To ensure accuracy, always double-check this procedure.

1 A quick method of transferring angles in the field of view is to carefully align the pencil against the angle seen in the subject that is being drawn.

3 Another method is to hold the pencil extended as a horizontal and to judge the angle, or angles, against this horizontal.

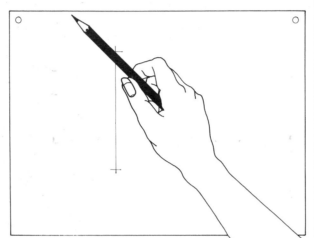

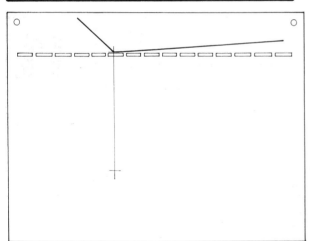

Yet another method of estimating angles is to make a circle with the thumb and the index finger through which the angles in the encircled field of vision are viewed with one eye closed. The angles are then compared with the hands of an imaginary clock face.

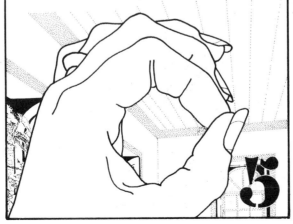

The horizontal is then recreated by the pencil on the drawing surface and, by comparison to it, the visualized angle or angles recorded. This method is especially useful for cubic objects and architectural space, but requires some practice in its use.

4

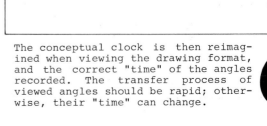

The conceptual clock is then reimagined when viewing the drawing format, and the correct "time" of the angles recorded. The transfer process of viewed angles should be rapid; otherwise, their "time" can change. **6**

5

Other Measuring Aids: Edges

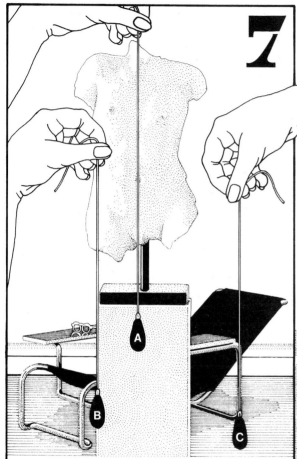

7

8 Another measuring device used by some artists is a 6" (150mm) square piece of clear acetate on which a square with 2" (50mm) sides is drawn with ink.

This is then held out into the visual field and employed as a basic unit of measure for assessing the proportion of shapes whose sight size and dimension are judged by comparison to those drawn on the acetate.

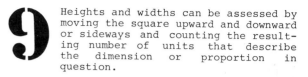

9 Heights and widths can be assessed by moving the square upward and downward or sideways and counting the resulting number of units that describe the dimension or proportion in question.

A simple device for establishing the relationship of objects and edges along a vertical plane is a plumb line. It is quickly made by attaching a weight, such as a bunch of keys, to a length of fine string. When held at arm's length in the field of view and sighted with one eye closed, it provides a portable and vertical grid line for: (a) establishing the central axis of an irregular shape; (b) checking the relative position of the edges of objects up and down the vertical plane; and (c) judging the relative edges of objects in the foreground and background of the subject.

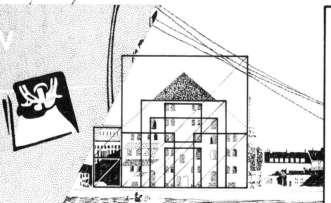

10 "Thinking in squares" is also a good technique when structuring the bare bones of a sketch or drawing. This technique of mental projection seeks squares within, around, and between the objects in view.

11 The squares are then reprojected, i.e., visualized either with or without the aid of the inked acetate square, onto the drawing format and recorded as the initial proportional framework for the ensuing drawing phase.

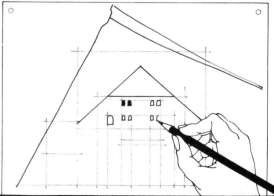

Drawing with a Grid

1

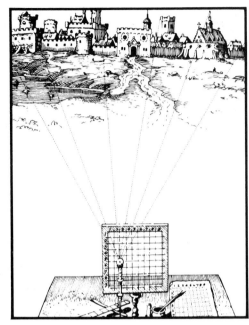

2

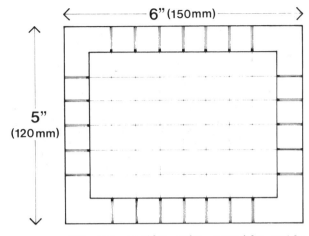

6" (150mm)

5" (120 mm)

You can easily make portable grids for sketching either by lashing, gluing, or taping cotton stretched across the window of a stiff-card viewfinder, or by filling a viewfinder window with a pregridded sheet of acetate.

3

The grid viewfinder fulfills two functions: it both frames the selected view and subdivides its contained format into units of squares--visual compartments that aid the transfer of shape and proportion.

Throughout the history of art and design, grids have lurked behind the structural composition of artwork and, indeed, have been utilized for the ordering of plans and facades of buildings. Grids are also used for transposing accurately observed objects in space onto a drawing board. This illustration --taken from a seventeenth-century woodcut-- shows how a portable grid, complete with its numbered squares, was set up in front of the view to be drawn. The artist or draftsman would peer through the viewing grid and, square by square, transfer the outline of observed shapes into the corresponding squares of the same predrawn grid on the drawing surface.

It is now thought that Western perspective was invented after someone looked through such a grid; recent research, in fact, has discovered that a building once stood on the very spot from which--it is calculated-- Brunelleschi made the first perspective drawing in Florence's Piazza del Duomo, in 1477. Furthermore, near this spot was a window, and it is speculated that he simply drew a grid on its glass to make a prototype of his famous drawing of the Baptistry.

4

Next, superimpose the drawing surface with an enlarged version of the grid drawn lightly and clearly with an F or HB grade pencil.

Using a B or 2B pencil to contrast the drawing with the grid, then plot the main outlines of the view--seen in relationship to the grid in the viewfinder--into the corresponding squares of the drawing-board grid. During the transfer process the portable grid should be held steadily and viewed without head movements.

5

Drawing with a Grid

6 Another proportional aid is to place a sheet of card with an ink-lined grid behind a still life group. Then, working on a same-size grid drawn on the drawing surface, you can confidently plot salient compositional outlines and their relationships and angles.

7

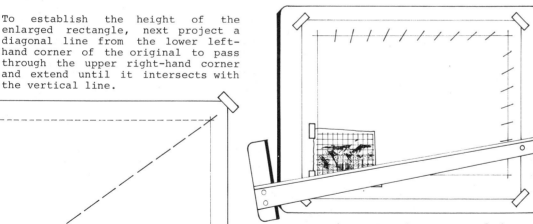

Grids are also useful tools for rescaling graphics, such as photographs, into drawings of a smaller or larger format. To enlarge a graphic, first superimpose the original with an accurate grid--its size of square being dictated by the required degree of accuracy in the transferred image.

8 Now tape the gridded original to the bottom left-hand corner of the drawing surface and, using a T square, extend its bottom line to the required length of the enlargement before projecting a vertical line from its end with a triangle.

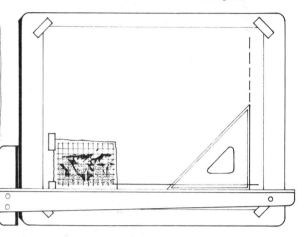

9 To establish the height of the enlarged rectangle, next project a diagonal line from the lower left-hand corner of the original to pass through the upper right-hand corner and extend until it intersects with the vertical line.

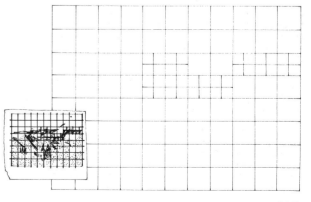

10 Now plot the squares of the enlarged grid by projecting lines from the lower left-hand corner of the original through each of the extremities of its vertical and horizontal grid lines until they intersect with the boundaries of the enlarged rectangle.

11 Finally, use the T square and triangle to complete the enlarged grid in readiness for guiding the accurate transfer of rescaled artwork. As smaller squares will increase accuracy of transfer, more intricate areas of the source image should be reduced in scale of grid, together with a corresponding reduction in the enlarged grid.

Drawing Boxes

The best introduction to object drawing --and the one adopted by most drawing and design courses--is the drawing of cubic forms, such as a cardboard box. In demanding a clear, linear execution, this kind of exercise instills an exacting observation of angles and proportion.

1

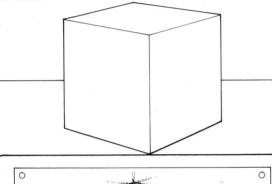

The basic principle behind the structure of each box drawing is, of course, two-point perspective. Extensions of the upper and lower converging lines find their respective vanishing points, which, in turn, pinpoint the horizon line, i.e., the line representing your eye level.

VP   VP

2

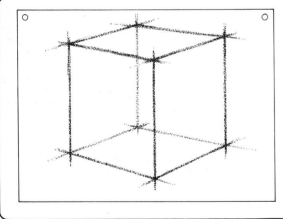

Begin by drawing individual cardboard boxes at sight size and viewed from a range of different overhead angles. Drawing at sight size means that you can take measurements directly in your field of vision using the pencil-thumb technique described on pages 74-75. Start each box drawing by establishing the near corner, with the knowledge that all vertical edges in the box will remain so in the drawing. Also, show all hidden lines in the drawing so that you sense the volume occupied by each box, and transfer angles of converging lines using one of the methods shown on page 76.

3

Graduate from individual boxes to stacked and grouped arrangements of boxes and cartons. Assume an eye level above the group and use a plumb line if necessary to plot the relationship of vertical edges in the vertical plane.

This introduction to drawing is important --not only because the act of drawing is the only way of improving your skills, but because "boxing" is a helpful tool in the proportioning of drawn objects.

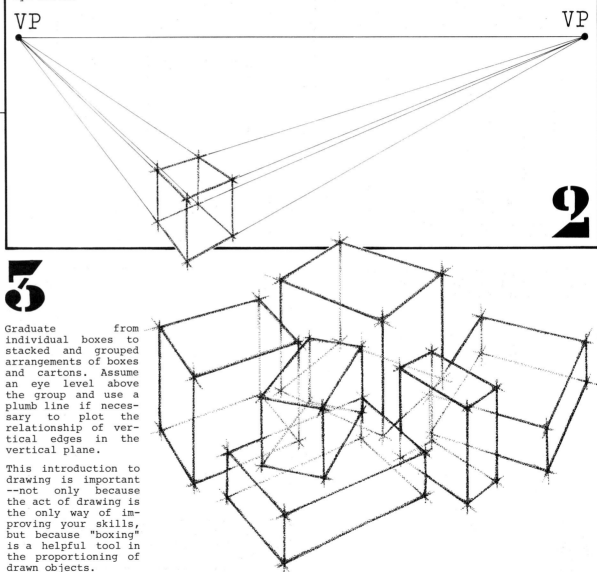

"Boxing" Drawings

1 Most three-dimensional forms have their geometric origin in the basic volumes of the cube, cone, cylinder, and sphere. Therefore, whenever you draw a three-dimensional object, it is helpful to first construct a container within which it will fit.

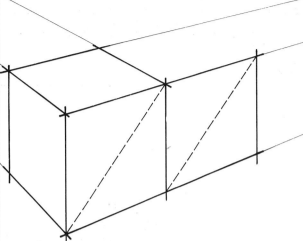

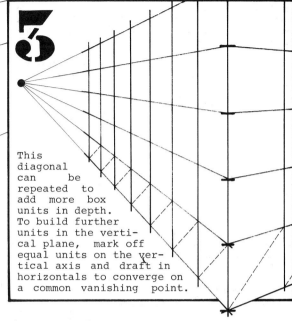

Construction "boxes" can be adapted and customized to accommodate a variety of forms. A single box is easily extended in perspective depth by drawing a diagonal line across its face.

2 If we draw a second diagonal parallel to the first, its intersection with the upper converging line finds the width of the next box.

3 This diagonal can be repeated to add more box units in depth. To build further units in the vertical plane, mark off equal units on the vertical axis and draft in horizontals to converge on a common vanishing point.

The curve of the face can now be drawn in freehand. Its shape is found when we pass the line through each of the four marked midpoints.

A cylinder is quickly fashioned if we initially box it within an imaginary cubic container of the same proportion.

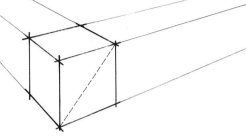

4

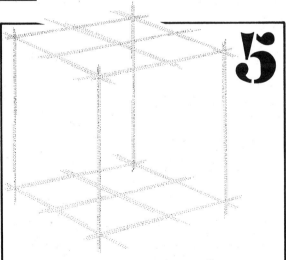

5 In two-point perspective, the cross-section of the cylinder will appear as an ellipse. To draw a circle in perspective, subdivide the upper and lower faces of the cubic container.

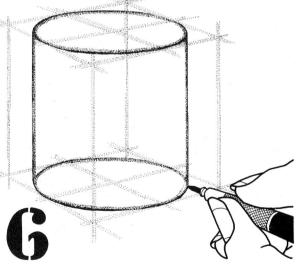

6

Construction as Drawing Technique

1

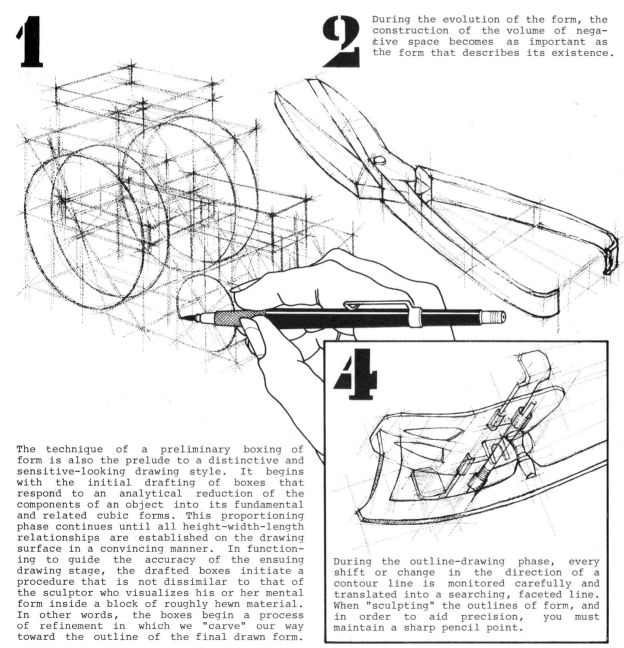

2 During the evolution of the form, the construction of the volume of negative space becomes as important as the form that describes its existence.

3

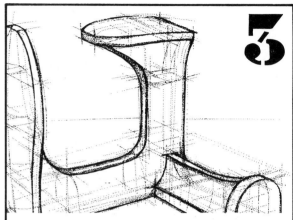

The drawing technique is also concerned with a changing line quality. For instance, subtle accents in the line weight result from increased pressure on the drawing instrument at critical points, such as points of overlap, connection, and intersection.

The technique of a preliminary boxing of form is also the prelude to a distinctive and sensitive-looking drawing style. It begins with the initial drafting of boxes that respond to an analytical reduction of the components of an object into its fundamental and related cubic forms. This proportioning phase continues until all height-width-length relationships are established on the drawing surface in a convincing manner. In functioning to guide the accuracy of the ensuing drawing stage, the drafted boxes initiate a procedure that is not dissimilar to that of the sculptor who visualizes his or her mental form inside a block of roughly hewn material. In other words, the boxes begin a process of refinement in which we "carve" our way toward the outline of the final drawn form.

4 During the outline-drawing phase, every shift or change in the direction of a contour line is monitored carefully and translated into a searching, faceted line. When "sculpting" the outlines of form, and in order to aid precision, you must maintain a sharp pencil point.

5

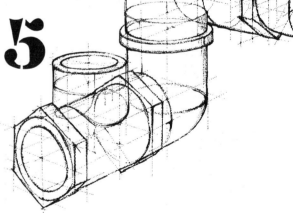

The final quality of the drawing stems from allowing its preliminary measurements and hidden guidelines to remain as part of its impression--their ghostlike presence appearing to reinforce its structural process and the illusion of depth.

The examples of drawings on this page are taken from the basic design course at Ulm, Germany.

Cross-Sectional Slicing

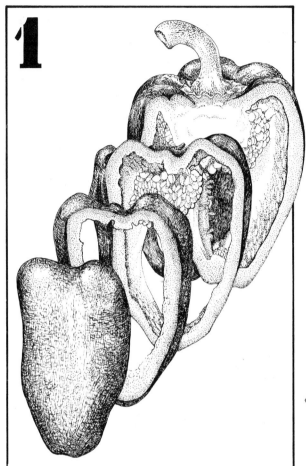

In operation, the slicing drawing technique aims to respond to the mental understanding of curved volumes. Probe lines are established that wrap the contour at selected points to create a preparatory hidden line structure that acts as an armature for the subsequent drawing.

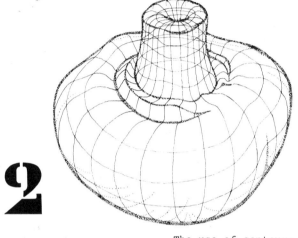

The slicing technique necessitates an awareness of the behavior of circular sections in relation to your point of view. For instance, when sectioning regular cylindrical forms, notice that their elliptical slices become progressively shallower in perspective as they approach your eye level.

Another construction technique in drawing is the conceptual "slicing" of, essentially, cylindrical, tubular, and rounded forms. In "seeing" through and around objects, this approach adopts a kind of X-ray vision to make an analytical sequence of probing slices that progressively monitors contour changes along and through a form. The best means of understanding this technique is to literally chop through a variety of different organic forms, such as zucchini, carrots, pears, peppers, mushrooms, etc., and make a contour drawing of each slice.

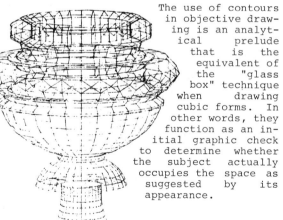

The use of contours in objective drawing is an analytical prelude that is the equivalent of the "glass box" technique when drawing cubic forms. In other words, they function as an initial graphic check to determine whether the subject actually occupies the space as suggested by its appearance.

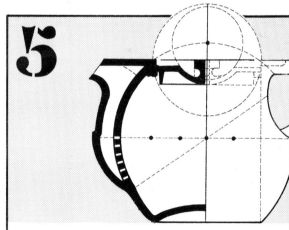

Experience with this kind of X-ray vision in object drawing prepares the way for an understanding of the role of the sectional cut in design--a device that slices through the space of ideas so that, once the cutaway portion is "removed," visual access is gained to internal cells.

Line Quality, Type, and Technique

The quality of line is an important aspect of drawing. For instance, if our drawings were comprised entirely of lines with the same thickness and intensity, their impression would appear to flatten the sensation of depth and solidity.

Therefore, when using continuous lines, encourage them to respond to a changing pressure that allows them to "breathe" in response to the contour of edges and to the nature of volumes they attempt to define. Line sensitivity results from an anchoring pressure at each end of their run, with a resulting elasticity of tension along their trajectory.

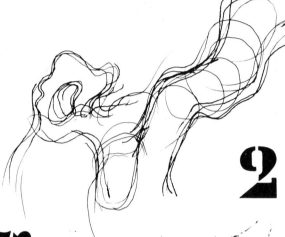

Broken-line techniques use vigorously applied short stabs of line that, when organized into clusters, perform the double function of simultaneously indicating edge and volume. The vitality of this line technique is harnessed to the play of light on form--edges being implied rather than defined. In the resulting drawing, the eye uses the given information to fill in any missing outlines.

As each plane receives its own amount of light, the insertion of shading becomes a natural extension of the preliminary line drawing.

Another version of the broken-line technique is generated from an analytical reduction of faceted edges. This technique is of interest because it not only reflects an observational "carving" of form as line . . .

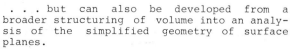

. . . but can also be developed from a broader structuring of volume into an analysis of the simplified geometry of surface planes.

84

Objective Drawing: Camera

1

Try the following freehand drawing technique to construct and render an object, such as a camera. Begin lightly in pencil after assuming a three-quarter view and positioning yourself about 2' (600mm) away from its form. Draw at sight size, with the drawing paper on a firm support. Using the pencil-thumb measuring method, start by identifying the components of a basic box construction. Remember that your close proximity to the subject will necessitate that dimensions be sighted and with your arm constantly returning to the same locked and crooked position.

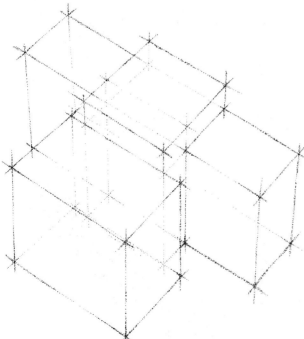

After establishing the two main construction boxes for the camera body and lens, devise an arrangement of appropriately sized boxes to guide the fashioning of the viewfinder housing and its connection with the lens.

2

Now develop the faceting of the viewfinder housing . . .

3

. . . and continue by finding the angles at the corner of the camera body and by constructing the cylindrical barrel of the lens within its boxed container.

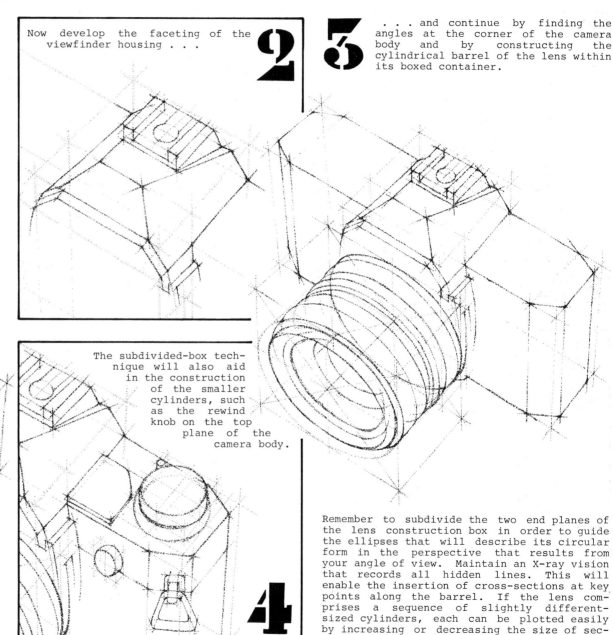

4

The subdivided-box technique will also aid in the construction of the smaller cylinders, such as the rewind knob on the top plane of the camera body.

Remember to subdivide the two end planes of the lens construction box in order to guide the ellipses that will describe its circular form in the perspective that results from your angle of view. Maintain an X-ray vision that records all hidden lines. This will enable the insertion of cross-sections at key points along the barrel. If the lens comprises a sequence of slightly different-sized cylinders, each can be plotted easily by increasing or decreasing the size of sectioned boxes around the central axis.

Objective Drawing: Camera

The seemingly complex grouping of the film-advance lever, the film-speed dial, and the shutter release can also be organized within a series of customized containers.

If in doubt, you should make a trial construction container to the side of the drawing before transferring its experience back into the main image.

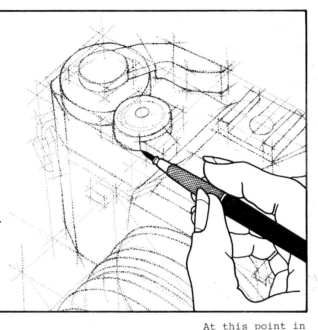

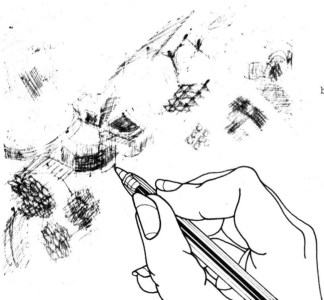

At this point in the drawing sequence, you should have achieved a carefully proportioned drawing with enough information to begin rendering in another medium, such as ballpoint pen. Begin the rendering phase by experimenting with a palette of trial techniques that aim to simulate the range of polished, textured, and nonreflective surfaces on the camera.

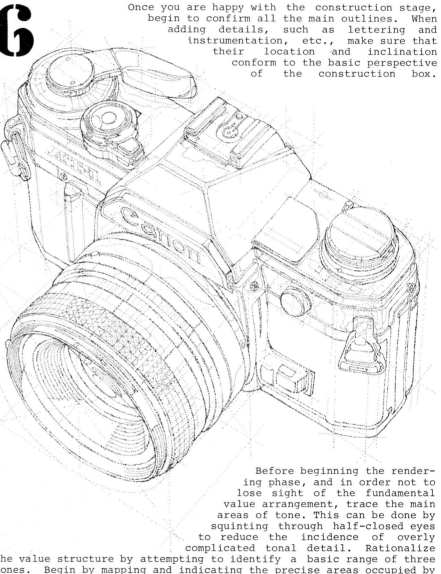

Once you are happy with the construction stage, begin to confirm all the main outlines. When adding details, such as lettering and instrumentation, etc., make sure that their location and inclination conform to the basic perspective of the construction box.

Before beginning the rendering phase, and in order not to lose sight of the fundamental value arrangement, trace the main areas of tone. This can be done by squinting through half-closed eyes to reduce the incidence of overly complicated tonal detail. Rationalize the value structure by attempting to identify a basic range of three tones. Begin by mapping and indicating the precise areas occupied by the darkest values, and then record the location of the lightest values together with any highlights. This tonal analysis will separate out and isolate the intermediate tones. Remember that, although generated by form, the value system will not always follow corners and edges precisely. In other words, do not draw what you cannot see.

Objective Drawing: Camera

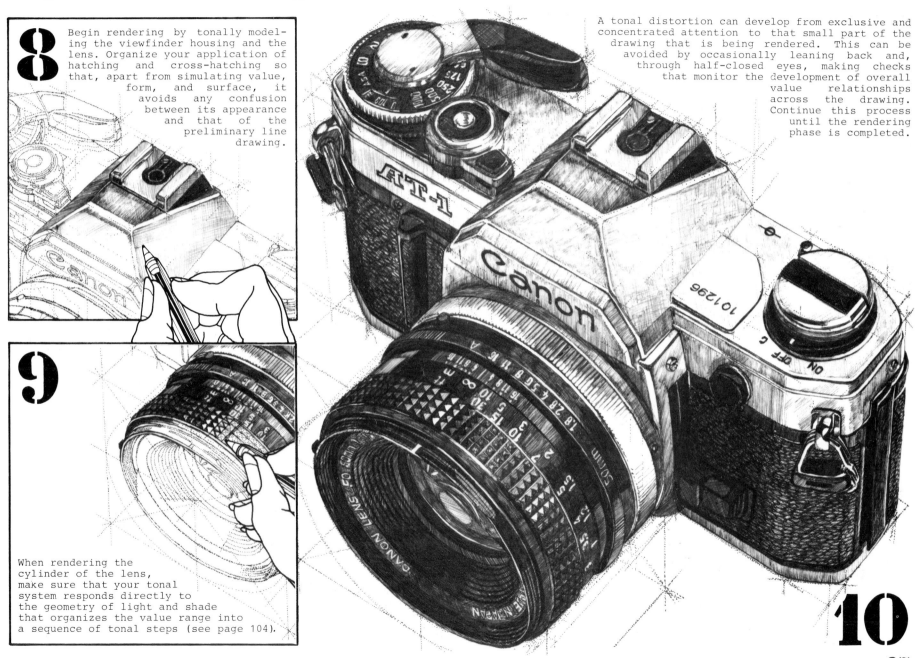

8 Begin rendering by tonally modeling the viewfinder housing and the lens. Organize your application of hatching and cross-hatching so that, apart from simulating value, form, and surface, it avoids any confusion between its appearance and that of the preliminary line drawing.

9 When rendering the cylinder of the lens, make sure that your tonal system responds directly to the geometry of light and shade that organizes the value range into a sequence of tonal steps (see page 104).

10 A tonal distortion can develop from exclusive and concentrated attention to that small part of the drawing that is being rendered. This can be avoided by occasionally leaning back and, through half-closed eyes, making checks that monitor the development of overall value relationships across the drawing. Continue this process until the rendering phase is completed.

Step-by-Step Still Life Drawing

Compose a group of the-matic objects into a still life set-piece that not only provides interesting views, or partial views, of indi-vidual elements but also collectively exploits the space between fore-ground and background. Position yourself close enough so that the area of your sight—size view of its massing corre-sponds to the size of your drawing paper.

The first series of steps will be concerned with the "under-draw-ing." Therefore, these should be worked lightly in pencil.

2

Step one is to plot the outer contour of the mass of objects against its interdependent net-work of negative shapes. During this stage you should force yourself to a selective concentra-tion on the analysis of the outer shape of the mass.

N.B.: Remember that shape has a positive and negative function and that an additional and singular concentration on the plotting of nega-tive shapes will act as a proportional check on their positive counter-parts.

13

Next, identify the outlines of indi-vidual objects within the mass. Care-fully trace the points of overlap between nearer and farther forms. As you know, overlap is a crucial depth cue and its incidence brings a degree of visual tension into the spatial illusion.

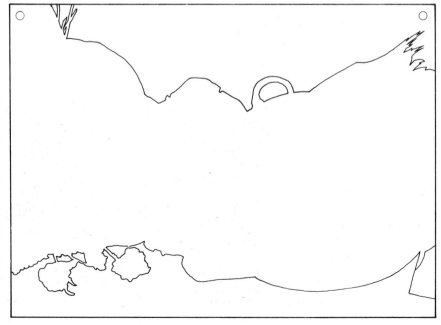

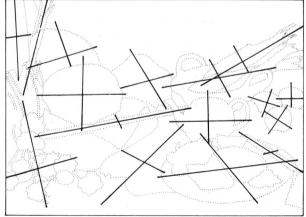

Now insert the main axes of all the dominant three-dimensional forms in the composition (if you extend these axes to the limits of your format, you identify the directional and spatial structure of your composi-tion).

4

Step-by-Step Still Life Drawing

Using the boxing technique for cubic and irregular forms, and the cross-sectional slicing technique for rounded forms, construct a guiding linear armature for each of the objects. After you have checked the under-drawing for accuracy, you have completed the first stage in the drawing process.

6 The next step is to add the first tentative layer of tonal value. Begin by emphasizing edges of stronger contrast and, with one eye on the actual appearance of value relationships in the still life group, remember to allow a decreasing tonal emphasis to encourage a sensation of space between foreground and background.

7 In your development of value rendering, recognize and respond to a precise mapping of the areas of shade and shadow. Avoid the mental separation of objects and the attendant tendency to draw edges that you cannot see. In other words, force yourself to record only what you see rather than what you know is in front of you.

5

Introduce a shading system that also responds to pattern and surface texture. At this stage, allow your shading to follow form, i.e., in a manner that emphasizes either the fullness or the flatness of its contour.

9

8

The drawing ends when you feel that you have graphically exhausted your perception of the group of objects. Finally, resist the temptation to use an eraser, and allow all your construction lines to remain as part of the final impression of the drawing.

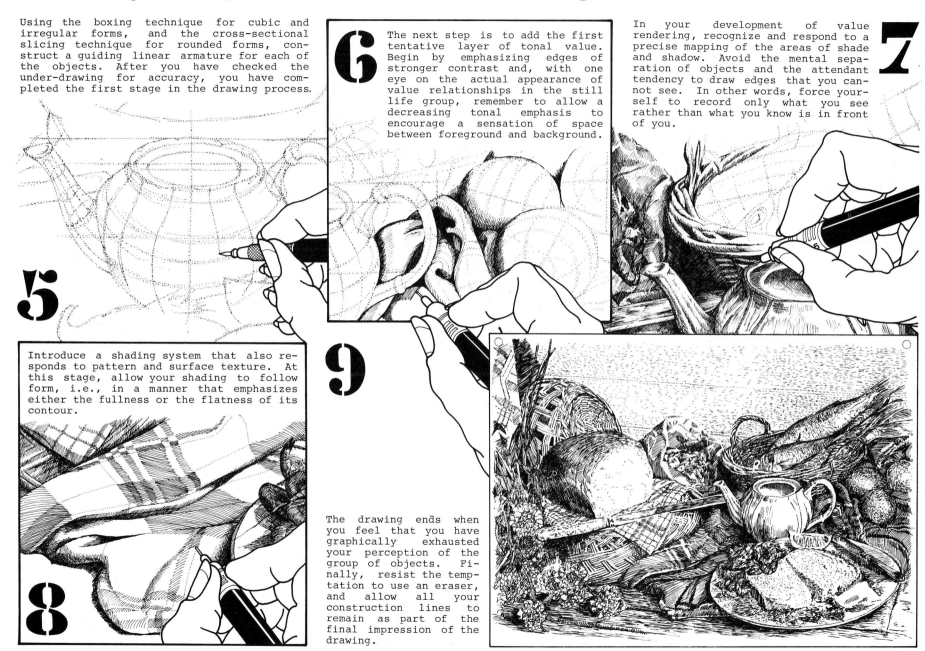

Drawing Buildings

1 When making drawings of buildings, aim to study a space defined by architecture rather than concentrating on a single facade or on making a "portrait" of an individual building. Therefore, seek a subject with a clear spatial structure, such as an urban "corridor" or a "framed" outdoor space. Also, select a view with good tonal variation and textural variety, as well as one that clearly exploits foreground, middleground, and background.

Work in pencil or pen on paper supported by a lightweight drawing board or in a sketchbook with a firm backing. Before commencing, spend some time examining the view and determine how much of your visual field you wish to include in the drawing. This decision--aided by your viewfinder--might necessitate some adjustment in your distance from the subject matter. Draw at sight size, and begin the initial stages of the drawing in fine or faint lines.

2 First, identify the main horizontal and vertical edges of the dominant forms within your selected view, and establish this simple geometry on the drawing paper. As these preliminary guidelines will act as the basic structure of the drawing, use the pencil-thumb measuring technique to cross-check its accuracy.

3 Next, identify the shapes of the main forms. "Hang" their contours around the previously established natural grid. By dividing the format into manageable areas, you simplify the process of relating various components of the basic formal pattern.

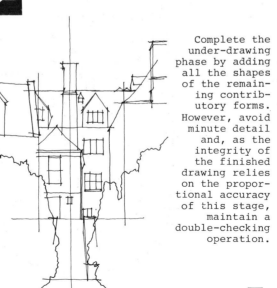

4 Complete the under-drawing phase by adding all the shapes of the remaining contributory forms. However, avoid minute detail and, as the integrity of the finished drawing relies on the proportional accuracy of this stage, maintain a double-checking operation.

5 When recording angles, employ one of the transfer aids listed on page 76. First, establish angles that are parallel to your line of vision. The location of the main upper and lower angles and their projection back into the space of the drawing will find the eye level and the vanishing point. These, in turn, will inform on the inclination of all related subsidiary angles.

Drawing Buildings

6 At this stage you can begin to develop the under-drawing into an overlay of detail and value. Rather than consider erasing parts of the preparatory line drawing, allow it to take part in and submerge beneath the ensuing drawing stages.

To avoid becoming overpreoccupied with an excessive elaboration of the value pattern, isolate the main areas of tone by squinting at the view through half-closed eyes. This will eradicate detail and "reduce" the pattern to its basic structure.

9 Detailing can continue, this time by inserting the texture of dominant surfaces. Avoid a stereotyped response by concentrating on the effect of light, i.e., the detailed indication of shade and shadow.

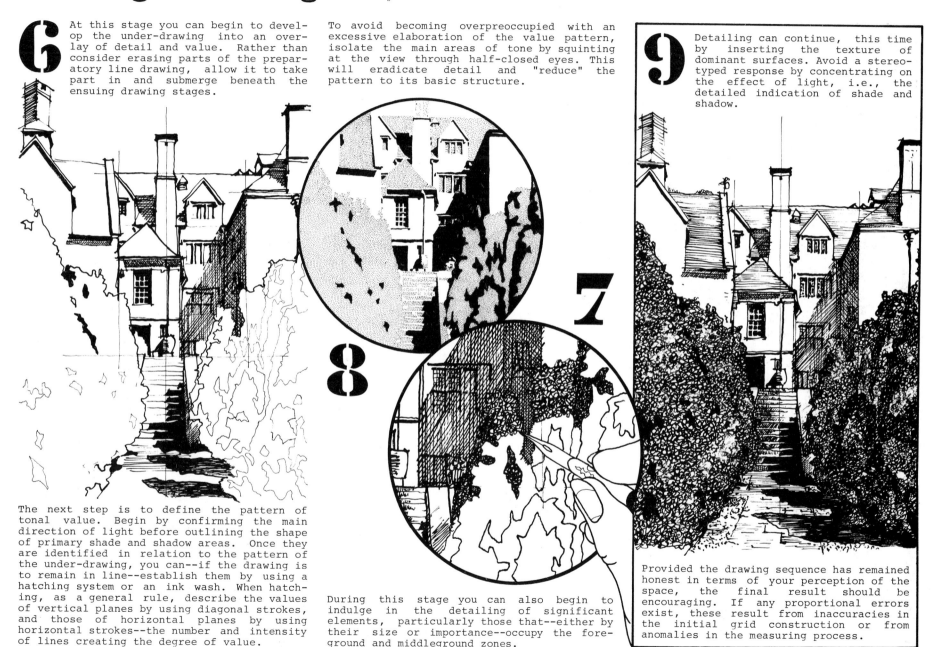

The next step is to define the pattern of tonal value. Begin by confirming the main direction of light before outlining the shape of primary shade and shadow areas. Once they are identified in relation to the pattern of the under-drawing, you can--if the drawing is to remain in line--establish them by using a hatching system or an ink wash. When hatching, as a general rule, describe the values of vertical planes by using diagonal strokes, and those of horizontal planes by using horizontal strokes--the number and intensity of lines creating the degree of value.

During this stage you can also begin to indulge in the detailing of significant elements, particularly those that--either by their size or importance--occupy the foreground and middleground zones.

Provided the drawing sequence has remained honest in terms of your perception of the space, the final result should be encouraging. If any proportional errors exist, these result from inaccuracies in the initial grid construction or from anomalies in the measuring process.

Upside-Down Drawings

One of the recurrent frustrations for beginners is the inability to draw accurately. This problem can stem from the impact of past experience on our perception of visual information--a perceptual superimposition that can override any potential freshness of observation. In other words, we tend to draw what we think--or "know"--we see, rather than respond directly to the actual information being perceived. In her book Drawing on the Right Side of the Brain, Dr. Betty Edwards suggests that the left and right cerebral hemispheres of the brain can come into conflict during the act of drawing. For instance, the left side of the brain is the seat of logic and rational deduction, while the right side is efficient at processing abstract, nonverbal information and at handling spatial pattern, texture, and value. However, when we make an objective drawing, the search for proportional accuracy in pictorial representation can be thwarted by the dominance of the verbal, left side of the brain, which tends to rationalize our visual understanding of form and space into stereotyped responses.

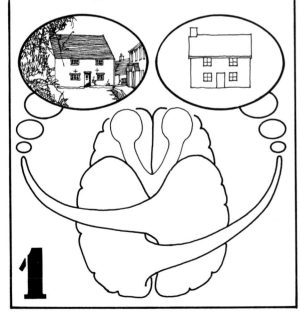

1

Dr. Edwards recommends a proven drawing exercise that can circumvent this problem. This is the production of an upside-down drawing made from a photograph selected for its richness of value and variegation of shape and pattern.

2

The fact that the brain cannot fully grasp the figurative meaning of the image frees the right side of the brain to apply its observational prowess and make a singular response to an abstraction of proportion and shape.

4

Because the photograph is retained in an inverted position, the drawing should develop a spirited and free interpretation of its pattern of shapes, lines, and values.

3

This inverted method of drawing has been used to effect by some Super-Realist painters. However, its execution can build confidence in beginners, for the final drawing, when righted, can convey a refreshingly honest and accurate graphic response.

5

5 DESIGN GRAPHICS

Process Graphics

The process of design generally begins with conceptual graphics, i.e., ideograms, symbols, and words that transfer to paper ideas that are visualized fleetingly in the dimensionless space of the mind's eye. Process graphics occur when ideas become so complex that they have to be externalized for clarification, assessment, and development. This externalization usually involves a language of abstraction in which descriptive hieroglyphics and annotation combine to chart the potential relationships between concept and reality. The newly transmitted idea will often appear as a constructive doodle that becomes the basis of a two-way dialogue between idea and mode of expression--a process that alternates until the creative process is exhausted.

1

2

During this process, ideas can become turned, surgically dismembered, enlarged, and mutated. Their generative marks act as positive-negative fields in which implied space and form are "read" simultaneously.

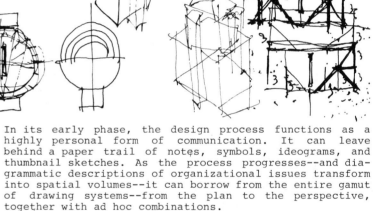

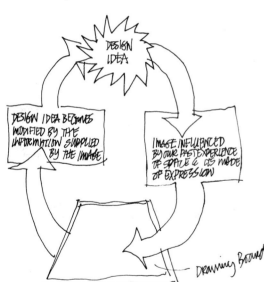

Through appropriate structuring, the diagram may generate different notions, or states of mind, in the viewer. However, these different notions, or states of mind, are susceptible to three factors that are also rooted in the designer's mind: familiarity with the mode of expression; the amount of information that the diagram supplies; and, embracing all, a previous experience of three-dimensional space.

Hitherto considered as an essentially private process, diagrams have recently been in the limelight. This is because, apart from chronicling the design sequence, they allow a shared and fascinating insight into the design route. As a result, generative graphics tend to be retained and used for a new role in communication.

The graphics above depict the work of Aldo Rossi (A), Robert Venturi (B), Charles Moore (C), and Michael Graves (D).

In its early phase, the design process functions as a highly personal form of communication. It can leave behind a paper trail of notes, symbols, ideograms, and thumbnail sketches. As the process progresses--and diagrammatic descriptions of organizational issues transform into spatial volumes--it can borrow from the entire gamut of drawing systems--from the plan to the perspective, together with ad hoc combinations.

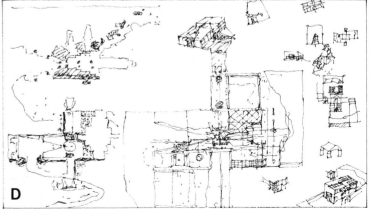

The Mechanics of Diagrams

In order to develop an effective design model and facilitate the evolution of ideas, you can employ a variety of diagram types--each with its own potential and conceptual set of rules that aid decision-making. For example, the matrix is a two-dimensional grid used to coordinate the relative importance of design elements. Once identified, the elements are listed across the top and/or down the side of the grid so that a hierarchical proximity between the elements is established.

The bubble diagram identifies the proximity and relative sizes of zones and activity elements. Often being fed by the information from a matrix, the bubble diagram represents the plan in embryo, for as they evolve, bubbles can metamorphose into shapes that herald the geometry of a later design solution.

Flow diagrams are four-dimensional in that they can identify change over time. They are often used to investigate direction, intensity, and the problems and possibilities of conflict that arise when movement is considered between one point and another.

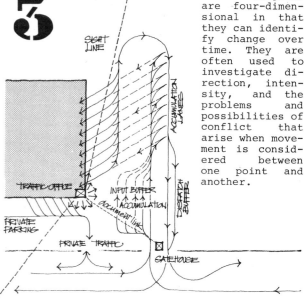

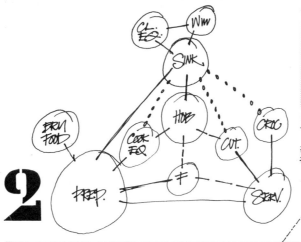

1

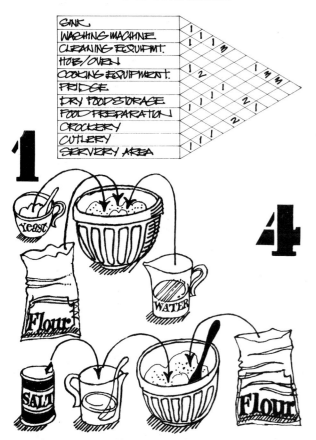

Operational diagrams embody another conceptual model that aids the designer in visualizing change in time. They begin to explain the mechanics of an idea and how its elements are manipulated and transformed. Diagram based on an illustration by Derek Norman.

4

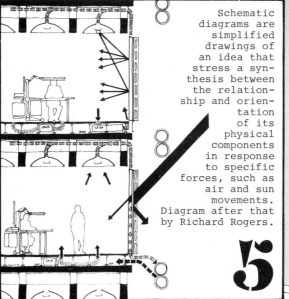

Schematic diagrams are simplified drawings of an idea that stress a synthesis between the relationship and orientation of its physical components in response to specific forces, such as air and sun movements. Diagram after that by Richard Rogers.

5

6

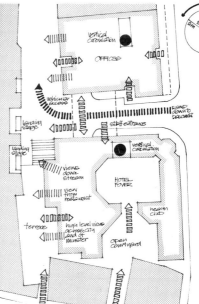

As an idea gains substance, the analytical diagram is used to identify and relate design constraints. Its main function lies in the investigation of the nature of existing conditions. In other words, it compares and evaluates a completed design against its original intention.

2

Diagrams as Analytical Drawings

1 According to the designer Keith Albarn, a diagram is evidence of an idea being structured--it is not the idea but a model of it, intended to define its characteristic features. It is a form of communication that increases the pace of development or allows an idea to function and develop for the thinker while offering the possibility of transfer of an idea or triggering of notions. To experience the diagram in action, experiment with the graphic communication of the following concepts:

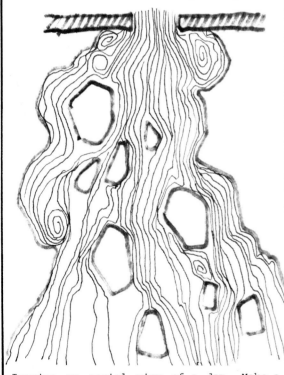

Imagine an aerial view of a dam. Make a plan of the dam holding back its contents from a dry canyon. The dam suddenly bursts and its waters gush into a dry, rock-filled river bed. Diagram the action of the rushing water as it floods around the rocks and into the canyon.

Diagram the operational sequence of how to tie a shoelace, a necktie, or a knot, or how to replace a blade in a cutting knife or a bit in a hand drill. Rationalize the sequence of events into a clear series of graphic stages.

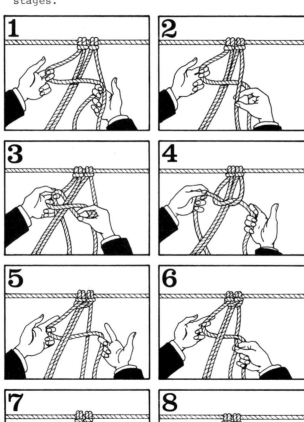

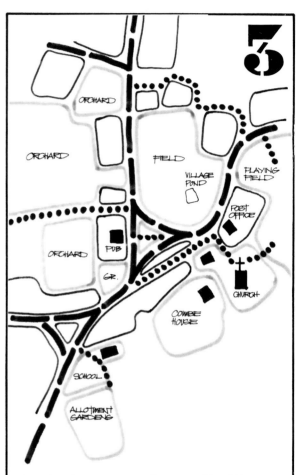

Diagram the anatomy of a small village or neighborhood. This "doodle" could schematically identify the shape and size of its interrelated working parts. For example, its spatial mechanism might comprise a "nerve center" or "heart" (bar, church, marketplace, crossroads); "lungs" (village green, playground, piazza, park); "arteries" (footpaths, waterways, road systems); any "distinguishing marks" (monuments, trees, tall chimneys, steeples); etc. Make sure that the component "bubbles" of your diagram are big enough to carry labeling.

Diagrams as Analytical Drawings

Using a flow diagram, track and superimpose a sequence of interrelated movement patterns between major activity centers within a room. For example, you could plot your movement patterns in the bedroom between bed, closet, door, window, radio, mirror, etc.

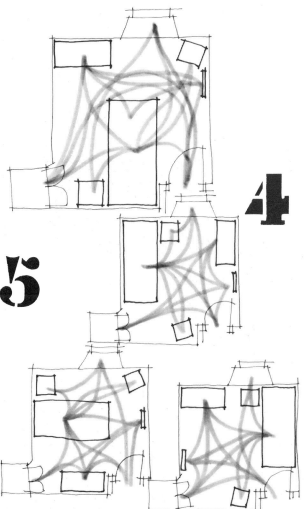

Using further diagrams, attempt to economize on the amount of movement by improving the spatial relationship between the objects in the bedroom.

The next diagramming experience takes us outside. Standing in the middle of an urban space and, while slowly rotating on the spot, trace a line that, in plan, symbolizes the limits of your all-around vision at eye level. Obviously, the parameters of your plan will be governed by the relative locations, directions, and heights of surrounding objects that interrupt the extent of your revolving point of view. You will discover that the plan line is liable to shoot out between gaps to distant points in the visual field--allow these to bleed off the edge of the drawing format. In completing its circuit, the continuous line will appear as a space bubble with your mind's eye at its center.

Now move to another point in the same outdoor space and produce a second spatial diagram. Comparison between the two bubbles will highlight how different one spatial experience is from another.

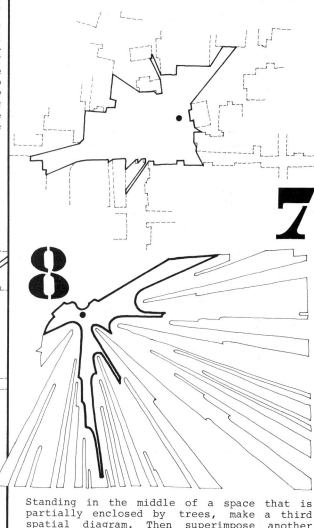

Standing in the middle of a space that is partially enclosed by trees, make a third spatial diagram. Then superimpose another spatial diagram, but this time using a bubble that predicts the change in its visual parameters in another season, say, in winter, when trees are without foliage.

The Vocabulary of Diagrams

1

Although diagramming is seen as an intensely personal form of visual communication, there are some aspects of its design language that are worth noting. Essentially, diagramming enlists the figure-ground illusion, i.e., a language of hierarchy in which a line can separate two ideas. A basic vocabulary for diagrams is discussed in Edward T. White's book Space Adjacency Analysis. Here, he outlines a hierarchical coding system that, in the context of bubble diagrams, harnesses embryonic spatial concepts to a lucid and efficient language of notation.

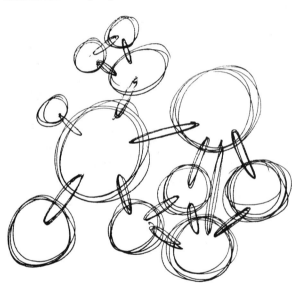

For example, the placement of the conceptual components of an idea plays an important role in the graphic model. This refers to proximity in which elements that are closer display more positive relationships than elements that are more separated. Discrimination between the importance of elements can be further indicated by a line-weight emphasis and, especially, by size--the volume of individual bubbles reflecting proportionally the relative areas of the spaces they characterize.

2

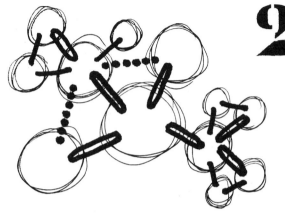

The connections between the elements follow another hierarchical system of notation that clearly expresses distinction between primary, secondary, and tertiary links. For instance, tenuous connections can be shown with dotted or dashed lines, desirable links with unbroken lines, and vital links with bold or double-lined bar connectors.

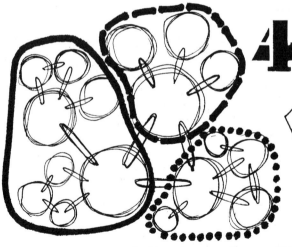

As the patterns of diagrams evolve, additional layers of information may be superimposed, such as the zoning, or classifying, of the nucleus into related clusters of function. Again, to avoid confusion, this elaboration should respond to a clear visual hierarchy of line weight, line type, or color.

The design implications of connecting lines are a most crucial element of a diagram and, in the notation suggested by White, thickness is more important than length. However, a useful alternative is the deployment of a hierarchical color-coding. In his promotion of color over monochrome, Le Corbusier once informed students that ". . . color will come to your rescue."

3

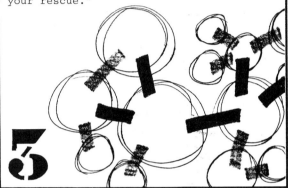

4

5

Also, as complexity increases, the mechanism of the diagram may be subject to additional symbols that investigate more detailed levels of adjacency and movement. However, as the diagram matures, an emphasis on its lucidity must be maintained.

98

Ideograms and Tactile Diary

This exercise is suggested as a means both of developing a personal notation and of testing its powers of communication as an abstract design language. Its origin lies in the design teaching of Johannes Itten, but its value is as relevant now as it was in the Bauhaus of the 1920s. Within a series of sixteen frames, graphically communicate each of the following contrasting concepts: high-low, up-down, heavy-light, flying-falling, vertical-horizontal, over-under, fast-slow, transparent-opaque, hard-soft, order-chaos, rough-smooth, straight-bent, backward-forward, in-out, and advancing-receding. None of the images should refer to known objects, nor include words, but should attempt to communicate clearly each antonym in pure, abstract symbols together with the subtle differences between the sixteen concepts. On completion, invite someone who has no knowledge of the assignment to match a random list of the antonyms to your set of diagrams.

1

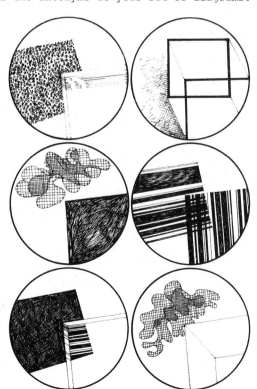

2

This exercise uses a storyboard, or comic-strip, format for the compilation of a tactile dictionary that is based on a consciously experienced chain of touch sensations within a room.

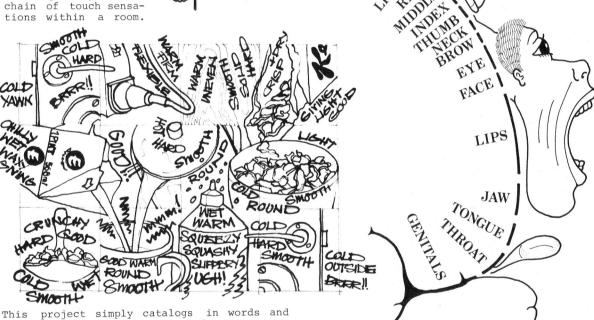

This project simply catalogs in words and pictures the variety of surface textures encountered by your body extremities during a short period. For example, your "dictionary" could monitor a sequence of sensations with respect to washing and grooming in the bathroom, dressing in the bedroom, or eating breakfast in the kitchen--all being early morning activities in which garments are less likely to impede the sense of touch. The aim of this exercise is to record various tactile events as words and diagrammatic sketches. In other words, a documentation of individual sensations associated with temperature, surface quality, substance, together with your subjective interpretation of each experience in terms of pleasantness and unpleasantness.

3

The latter exercise is concerned with retaining a focus on the sense of touch, which is ultimately experienced in a region of the brain that is different from our sense of sight. This is a "homunculus," i.e., a graphic representation that shows how much of the brain is devoted to sensation from various parts of the human body. This rather bizarre diagram remaps the human body using touch sensitivity to determine the importance--and hence, size--of each body member.

Diagrams in Communication

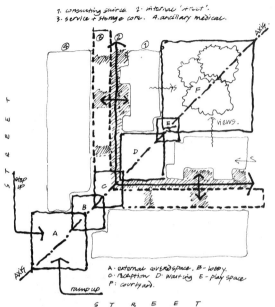

1. consulting suites. 2. internal 'street'.
3. service + storage core. 4. ancillary medical.

A. external covered space. B. lobby.
C. reception D. waiting E. play space
F. courtyard.

As analytical drawings, diagrams operate across the entire sequence of design and, in their generative form, can be employed for a public communication of ideas. Also, they are often enlarged and elaborated for the presentation of particularly intricate problems and solutions to groups of people.

This diagram is a concept plan based on the work of Denton, Tunley, Scott.

1 The essence of diagrams can also be found in a whole variety of working graphics. For instance, Henry C. Beck's classic subway map for London's underground system elevates the flow diagram into a highly sophisticated and, in its original form, color-coded graphic that is still in use over fifty years after its conception.

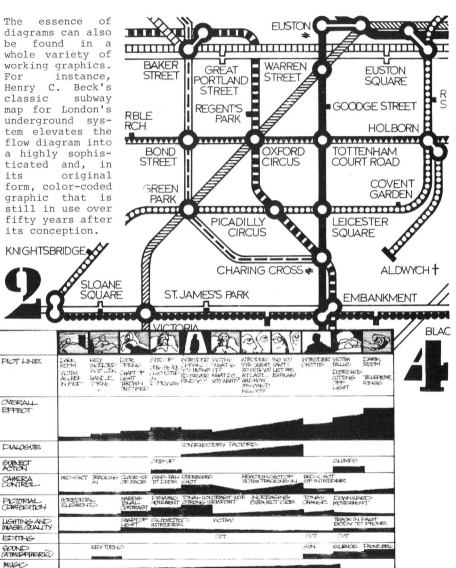

2

3

Meanwhile, from the world of product design, this analytical section functions as a schematic diagram that explains the behavior of energy patterns emanating from a light source and scattered in reaction to the design for a lampshade.

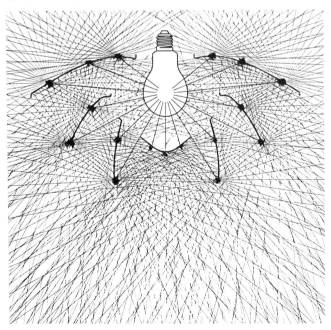

4

This is a movie storyboard that diagrams the action of a single scene from a television play. In marrying a sequence of contributory aspects, such as sound, image, mood, and light, etc., this comparatively simple graphic coordinates a host of complex and related information. In achieving this synthesis, this specialized drawing has its roots in the operational diagram.

Diagrams in Communication

Possibly the most frequent use of diagrams in communication at large comes in the form of statistical graphics: graphs, histograms, pie and bar charts, etc. This illustration by Geoff Sims for The Sunday Times of London combines a map tilted into pictorial space, with an attendant bar chart to convey its frightening statistics. Notice how the horrific content of its message is reinforced by the introduction of associated symbols that, in the form of the crosses, vary in size in relation to the figures they represent.

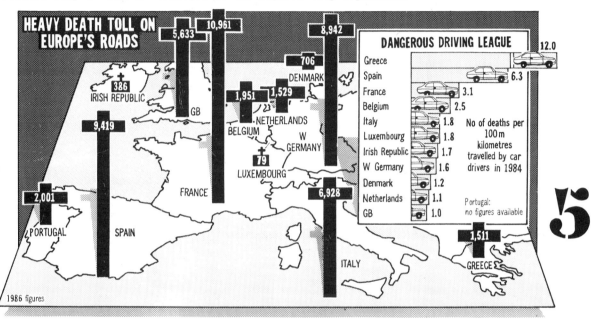

HEAVY DEATH TOLL ON EUROPE'S ROADS

1986 figures

DANGEROUS DRIVING LEAGUE

Greece	12.0
Spain	6.3
France	3.1
Belgium	2.5
Italy	1.8
Luxembourg	1.8
Irish Republic	1.7
W Germany	1.6
Denmark	1.2
Netherlands	1.1
GB	1.0

No of deaths per 100 m kilometres travelled by car drivers in 1984

Portugal: no figures available

REAGAN'S NIGHTMARE: HOW HELPING KUWAIT COULD DRAG AMERICA INTO CONFLICT

W Europe 2.20
US 0.60
Japan 2.60
Million barrels per day
Source: Wood Mackenzie

1 America tries to protect ships carrying oil to the west, even though little goes to the US

2 Kuwaiti tanker flying US flag hits Iranian mine

3 America launches air strike against Iranian naval base

4 Iranian terrorists hit back against US targets: hostages killed in Beirut

5 Reagan faces choice of surrender or war with Iran

This is another example of graphics reportage from the same newspaper, this time taken from an illustration by Phil Green. In employing a diagram with figurative images to sequence a series of events and place them within a geographic and economic context, this drawing shows another version of a four-dimensional operational diagram.

This analytical drawing is derived from the design work of Clino Castelli. Its manner of describing the impact of temperature, acoustics, daylight and electric light, and color on the volume of an existing architectural space represents a highly sophisticated type of schematic diagram.

An Introduction to Drafting

If we add an adjustable triangle, compass, flexible curve, ruler, and T square to our basic set of drawing instruments, we become equipped for a more mechanical form of drawing. However, when we enter this world of conventional graphics, there is no need--as is often the case with beginners--to abandon an understanding of form, surface, light, and space. At this point, apart from the additional drawing tools, the only thing that will change is the mode of the drawing. The following exercise is a useful vehicle for helping to familiarize yourself with the drawing equipment, to gain experience in simple drafting techniques, and to gain insight into the creation of convincing three-dimensional illusions in the nonperspective space of a simple projection drawing. Using a large drawing-board format, begin in pencil with the drafting of a spontaneous arrangement of five or more geometric and free-form shapes clustered around the near-center of the paper.

1 N.B.: Keep each shape discrete and separate from its neighbors. Also, with the aid of your drafting equipment, construct each shape clearly and cleanly.

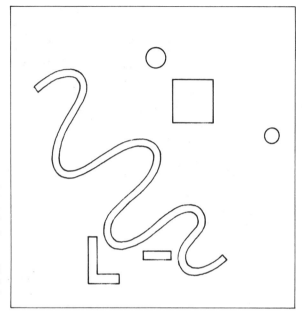

2 Using the triangle and T square, now project the corners and outer edges of each shape in a completely different direction and out to the limits of the format. All projected lines should remain parallel to the chosen direction of each respective shape.

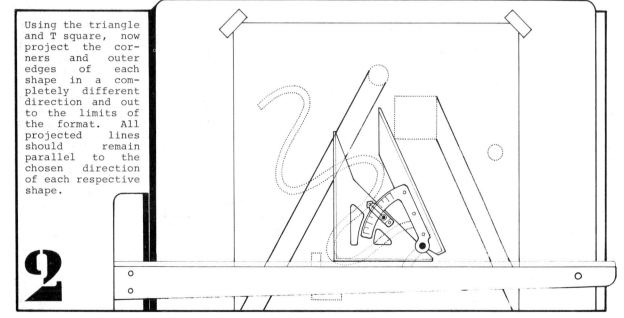

3 During the projection stage you should exploit the greatest possible variety of direction. This stage also necessitates decisions concerning near-far relationships of newly projected forms in terms of their sequence of overlap.

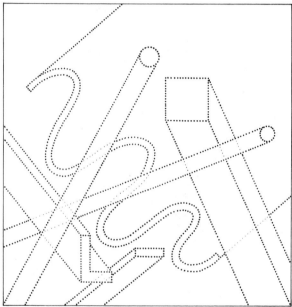

4 Having arrived at this point, we can see that our shapes have transformed into volumes whose forms--without the aid of any other depth cue--occupy a powerful three-dimensional space, an illusion confirmed only by the overlap depth cue. To further reinforce this illusion, we should now turn to rendering each form. However, in order to begin this stage, we first need to assume a direction of light.

An Introduction to Drafting

Begin your technical pen rendering on one of the simpler foreground objects, such as a form with a square section. Use a single-direction line system to reinforce its shaded plane--following either its length or its width.

At the end of the rendering stage, resist the temptation to ink in the outlines of the original shapes. In their new role as profiles of projected forms, they will simply be "painted in" by the perception of the viewer.

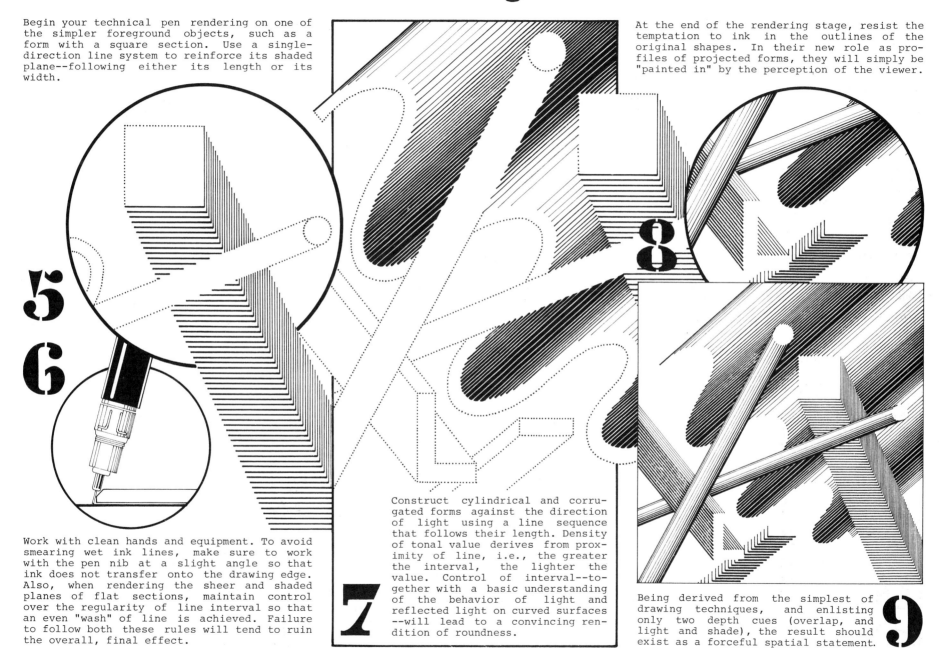

Work with clean hands and equipment. To avoid smearing wet ink lines, make sure to work with the pen nib at a slight angle so that ink does not transfer onto the drawing edge. Also, when rendering the sheer and shaded planes of flat sections, maintain control over the regularity of line interval so that an even "wash" of line is achieved. Failure to follow both these rules will tend to ruin the overall, final effect.

Construct cylindrical and corrugated forms against the direction of light using a line sequence that follows their length. Density of tonal value derives from proximity of line, i.e., the greater the interval, the lighter the value. Control of interval--together with a basic understanding of the behavior of light and reflected light on curved surfaces --will lead to a convincing rendition of roundness.

Being derived from the simplest of drawing techniques, and enlisting only two depth cues (overlap, and light and shade), the result should exist as a forceful spatial statement.

Design Rendering Techniques

1

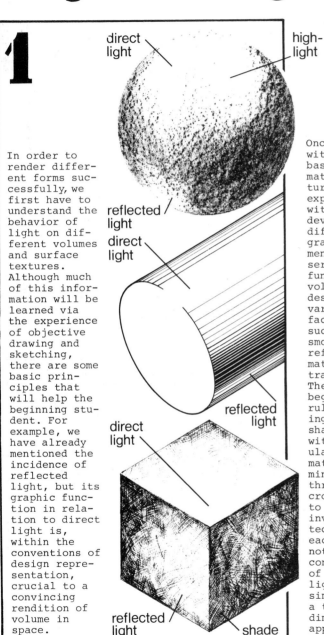

In order to render different forms successfully, we first have to understand the behavior of light on different volumes and surface textures. Although much of this information will be learned via the experience of objective drawing and sketching, there are some basic principles that will help the beginning student. For example, we have already mentioned the incidence of reflected light, but its graphic function in relation to direct light is, within the conventions of design representation, crucial to a convincing rendition of volume in space.

2

Once armed with this basic information, we can turn to experimenting with the development of different graphic treatments for a series of fundamental volumes as described by various surface finishes, such as rough, smooth, reflective, matte, and transparent. These can begin with a ruled hatching, or bar shading, and, with particular surface materials in mind, continue through cross-hatching to more inventive techniques. In each case, note the contribution of reflected light to the simulation of a three-dimensional appearance of solidity.

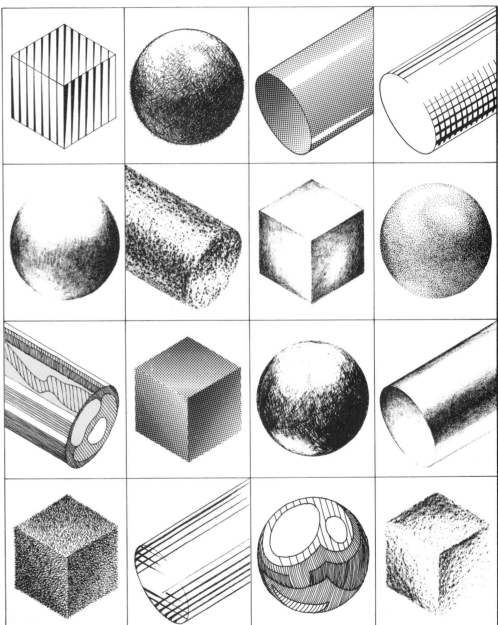

Design Drawing in Line

1

At the core of drawing is the line. Unaided or unembellished by shading, the pure line drawing has to function to express qualities of space, light, form, and surface. On the one hand, line drawings can be fresh and spontaneous--as in a sketch; on the other hand, they can be deliberate and exacting--as in a precision orthographic. When we describe space exclusively in line, we enlist a convention that is quite unrelated to our visual perception. However, we employ a medium that possesses great powers of communication.

2

A closer investigation of Mollino's line technique reveals a deliberate break in the line--especially at the tension points of overlap. Each break is made when the edge of a farther object apparently passes behind that of a nearer object --a technique that infers a degree of space between the two objects.

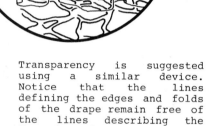

Transparency is suggested using a similar device. Notice that the lines defining the edges and folds of the drape remain free of the lines describing the forms beyond.

When Mollino drew orthographics, such as this plan, he retained many of the fluid qualities of his perspectives. Rather than descend into a mechanical technical drafting, his drawings retain a delightfully sensitive and sensuous delineation.

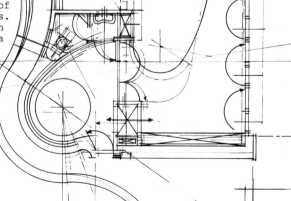

3

For example, this is a perspective drawing of a design for a studio, taken from one done in 1942 by the Italian designer Carlo Mollino. Notice the simplicity of his linework and the use of only two basic line weights. This self-imposed restriction is quite remarkable when we consider his achievement of transparency, texture, space, and light.

Design Drawing: Line into Tone

1

In this drawing taken from the sketchbook of graphic designer Milton Glazer, we see a line drawing in transition --from the fluid pen strokes on the left to their role in guiding a layer of hatched rendering on the right. Here, value is applied as a patchwork of tightly clustered groups of lines. Tonal variation is indicated via a varying pressure on the pen, while textural variation is suggested by the length, descriptive quality, and speed of the pen strokes.

By contrast, the pen drawings of architect Le Corbusier display a highly restrained use of tonal elaboration. His lines tend to remain virtually intact while an almost incidental layer of ticks, dots, and squiggles suggests rather than describes the surface textures of plaster, wood, and glass. Like Glazer's sketch, Le Corbusier's concept drawing conveys a freshness of vision (albeit of a space that exists only in the designer's mind)--a quality emanating from a total command of the medium.

2

This drawing demonstrates the marvelous potential of the pencil in suggesting space and light in orthographics. It is taken from the work of designer Giuseppi Zambonini, whose hallmark in design graphics is the employment of delightfully subtle accents of line weight and tone. For instance, notice the strengthening of lines in this interior floorscape as they approach the contours of the bathroom furniture. This visual trick emphasizes shadow to reinforce the figure-ground illusion. Also notice how the ends, corners, and intersections of the plan's sectional cut are intensified with a darker shading--a technique that simultaneously registers these critical points in the structure and "etches" the quality of contained space.

3

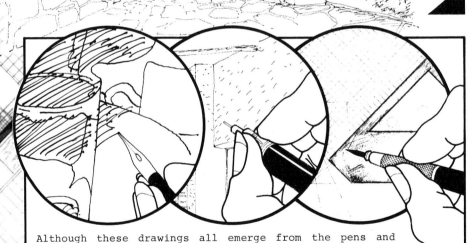

Although these drawings all emerge from the pens and pencils of quite different designers, they exhibit a common denominator, i.e., each style of rendering is applied in a left-to-right diagonal direction. Within the potential of the vast range of marks at the disposal of designers to personalize a rendering style, this simple directional technique is used both to avoid confusion with the line drawing and to instill an underlying sense of order in the finished drawing.

4

A Hint of Hatching

1

Functioning in a variety of roles in design drawings, hatching is a basic rendering technique that employs sets of parallel lines. At its most basic, hatching is used in town planning and architectural drawings for a simple figure-ground differentiation in small block plans. Either drawn in freehand or ruled, the resultant tonal value visually identifies mass from a surrounding void.

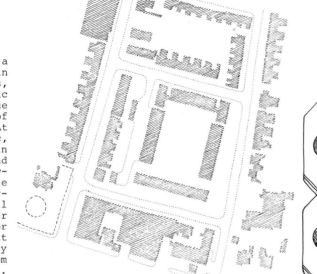

2 Usually associated with pen and pencil, hatching is much used in technical illustrations--especially those destined for reproduction. In this context, simple variations in line weight, proximity, and direction have the potential for describing form and the nature of its surface.

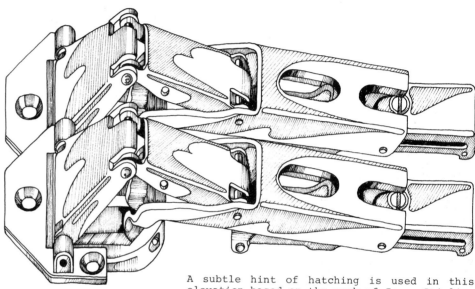

3

A specialized use of hatching is found in site plans, where, in following the trajectory of contour lines, continuous bands of parallel lines describe the topographical nature of landform.

A subtle hint of hatching is used in this elevation based on the work of James Stirling and Partner. Within a drawing comprising two line weights--broken and unbroken lines, ruled and freehand lines--minimal hatching indicates cast shadows that function to bring a sense of the third dimension.

4

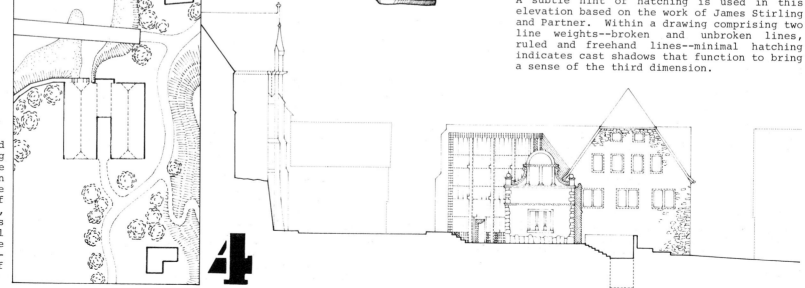

First and Third Angle Projection Drawing

Through the coordination of the plan and the elevation, orthographic projection drawing is a method of representing the many faces of an object on paper. Its basic principles are best understood if an object is visualized in relation to one of the four quadrants described by the imaginary intersections of transparent vertical and horizontal planes. Each quadrant provides the views for first, second, third, and fourth angle projections.

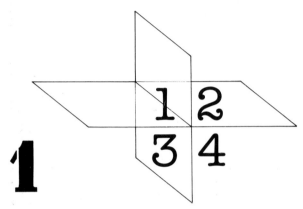

1

When the "shadows" are flattened out to fit onto drawing paper, we have the traditional layout of first angle projection with elevations above the plan.

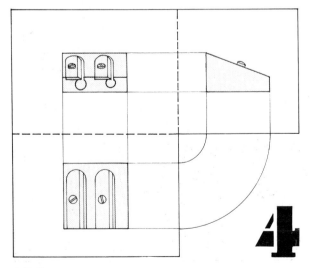

4

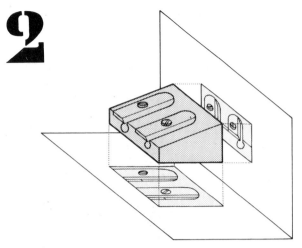

2

For instance, if we insert an object into the first quadrant and imagine its true-to-scale faces as projected shadows on the two planes, we see the basic relationship between the elevation (front view) and the plan (horizontal view).

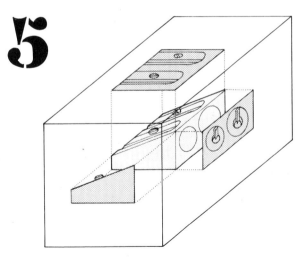

5

In third angle projection, the object is visualized through the transparent planes. In other words, this projection "reflects" true-to-scale information from each of the faces.

If two views are inadequate for more complex objects, an extension at right angles to the vertical plane is added to catch the "shadow" of its profile (end elevation). Notice that the information on all planes derives from the faces of the object that are nearest the viewer.

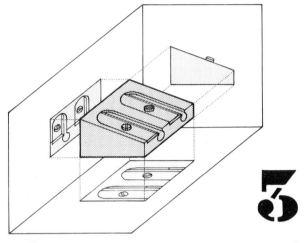

3

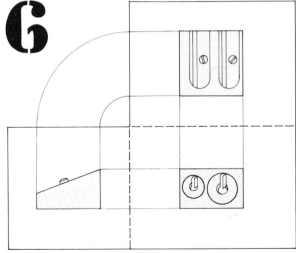

6

When third angle projections are flattened out onto the drawing surface, we find the most commonly used arrangement of plan and elevation in design.

Orthographic Scale

1

Orthographic drawings can be used to represent formal events as small as an electric plug and as large as a town. Therefore, the size of a drawing in relation to what it attempts to communicate is important. For example, the plan of a plug can be shown at same size, i.e., one-to-one. However, before a town plan can be accommodated on the same size sheet of paper, it has to be drastically shrunk conceptually, and may be drawn to a scale of 1 : 12,500.

1 : 1

1 : 12,500

2

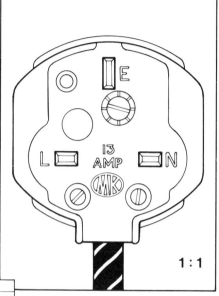

1/4" = 1'-0" (1:50)

1/8" = 1'-0" (1:100)

1/16" = 1'-0" (1:200)

1:500

In other words, the selection of scale for an orthographic drawing is a means of regulating the distance between the designer's eye (or mind's eye) and the size or degree of complexity of an object or a concept. In environmental design, floor plans are usually drawn to a scale of 1/4" = 1'-0" (1 : 50), or 1/8" = 1'-0" (1 : 100). Increasingly larger buildings and building complexes can be shrunk along decreasing scales of 1/16" = 1'-0" (1 : 200), or 1 : 500. Thus, in selecting scale, the designer not only regulates the distance of an idea but also regulates its graphic size so that it fits within the confines of the drawing board.

3

This table serves to remind the beginner of the degree of detail afforded by scaled size representation and of how familiar objects appear and, indeed, disappear along the conventional scales.

1 : 1250

1 : 200

1 : 500

1 : 100

1 : 50

1 : 20

Orthographic Points of View

A good way of understanding the roles of the plan, section, elevation, and paraline projection is via their collective ability to represent our conceptual movement about and through the space occupied by a design idea. In other words, each drawing mode contributes to a sequence of vantage points from which the designer can make a comprehensive examination of a developing form--either visualized in mental space or recorded in the dimensioned facets of its three-dimensional existence. For instance, the plan takes us above a form for a graphic aerial view of its completeness or, alternatively, for a glimpse of its interior hollowness resulting from a conventional slicing that removes its upper portion.

Our vantage point is brought down to earth by the section. In acting as a vertical version of the conventional plan, the section provides a head-on, cutaway view into the nature of inner space and its relationship with outer, surrounding space.

The elevation retains this frontal, horizontal viewpoint for a simulated eye-level view of external events. However, in order to complete our comprehension of more complex forms, we have to make a visual tour around the form so that changes in its "faces" can be monitored from, essentially, the four compass points.

In combining the plan with the elevation, the plan oblique provides a three-dimensional view seen from an angled overhead vantage point. The view results from rotating the true plan and projecting its vertical planes at the same scale.

45° 45°

In contrast to the plan oblique, the isometric projection responds to a viewpoint that is lower in relation to the ground plane. This is because the plan is tilted and seen as a foreshortened plane--the two true-length ground-plane axes both being angled at 30 degrees to provide a scaled view of the three planes but with equal distortion.

30° 30°

In presenting contradictory clues, the ambiguity of paraline drawings affords upper (bird's-eye) and lower (worm's-eye) viewpoints. This ambiguity is epitomized in Thiery's Figure, which, according to E. H. Gombrich, provides a dualism of viewpoint that represents the quintessence of Cubism.

110

Orthographic Side Effects

1

Isometrics are not used as vehicles for objective drawing but are more exclusively employed as "containers" for ideas. However, the distortion that would be encountered when transferring objective information into its "glass box" makes an interesting comparison with the transfer of concepts, because the latter, being in a fluid state, are possibly less resistant to the squareness of its configuration. For example, the difficulty experienced if we were to try to draw an organic object in isometrics is the same for nonrectilinear ideas. Therefore, the designer should be aware of the potential straightjacketing of nonconformist concepts.

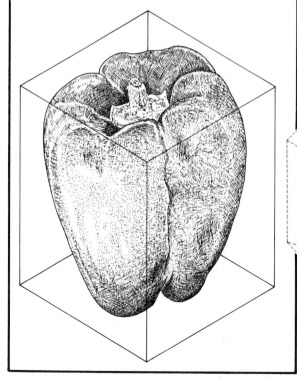

This conditioning toward "squareness"--an effect that relates to our apparent inability to visualize forms existing beyond the influence of the right angle--has been demonstrated by Victor Papanek. He describes an experiment in which design and nondesign students were asked to interpret information from this front and side elevation. Due to its ambiguity, two solutions are possible.

2

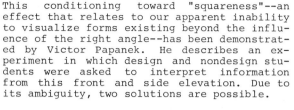

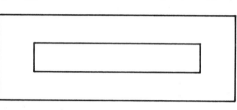

It has also been speculated that the current fascination with plan projections in architectural design has, in turn, influenced the "erosion" of the corners of buildings. Indeed, the work of many designers seems rooted in a drawing mode. For example, James Stirling's love of minimal, deadpan projections seems inextricably linked with the resultant design.

3

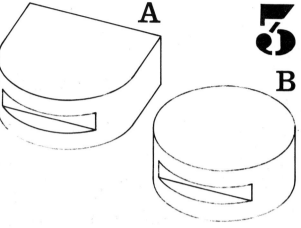

Papanek found that more designers failed to arrive at the more "elegant" solution (B) than those uninitiated into orthographics. Because of the lack of depth cues, the designers assumed that the elevations described a squareness or rectangularity--being unable to visualize alternative forms.

Similarly, Paul Rudolph's early buildings expose their inner cells with a sawn-off appearance that reflects his love of the cross-section. In the face of complex organic forms, some designers, such as Eero Saarinen and Louis Kahn, have supplemented drawing with three-dimensional modeling.

4

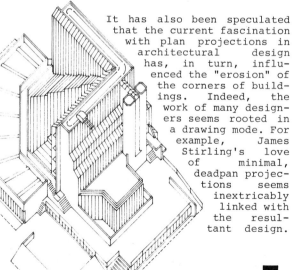

5

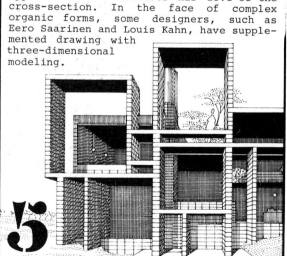

Depth Cues in Orthographics

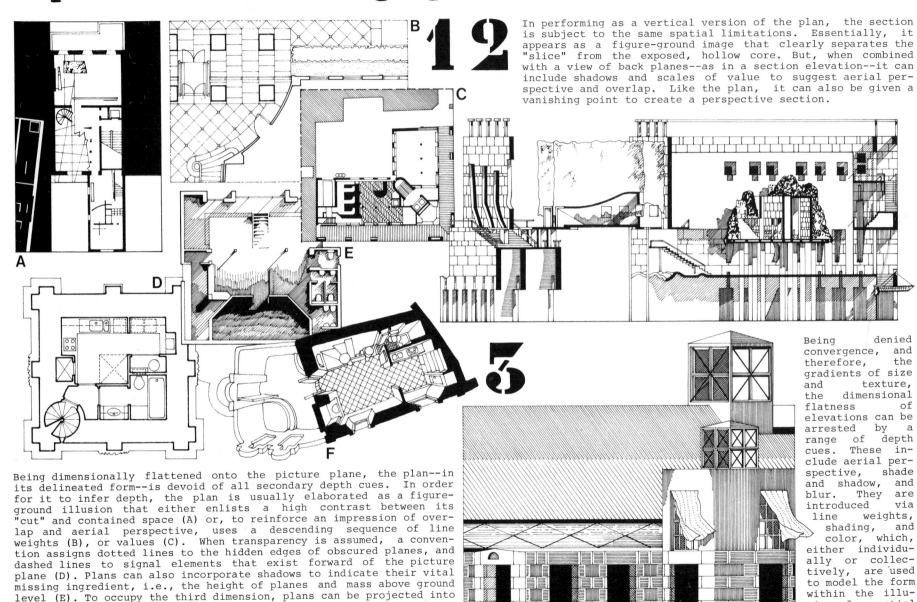

In performing as a vertical version of the plan, the section is subject to the same spatial limitations. Essentially, it appears as a figure-ground image that clearly separates the "slice" from the exposed, hollow core. But, when combined with a view of back planes--as in a section elevation--it can include shadows and scales of value to suggest aerial perspective and overlap. Like the plan, it can also be given a vanishing point to create a perspective section.

A C D E F 3

Being denied convergence, and therefore, the gradients of size and texture, the dimensional flatness of elevations can be arrested by a range of depth cues. These include aerial perspective, shade and shadow, and blur. They are introduced via line weights, shading, and color, which, either individually or collectively, are used to model the form within the illusion of a spatial setting. Drawing based on the work of Felim Dunne.

Being dimensionally flattened onto the picture plane, the plan--in its delineated form--is devoid of all secondary depth cues. In order for it to infer depth, the plan is usually elaborated as a figure-ground illusion that either enlists a high contrast between its "cut" and contained space (A) or, to reinforce an impression of overlap and aerial perspective, uses a descending sequence of line weights (B), or values (C). When transparency is assumed, a convention assigns dotted lines to the hidden edges of obscured planes, and dashed lines to signal elements that exist forward of the picture plane (D). Plans can also incorporate shadows to indicate their vital missing ingredient, i.e., the height of planes and mass above ground level (E). To occupy the third dimension, plans can be projected into the coordinates of the isometric or axonometric (see facing page), or be extruded into the convergence of an aerial perspective (F). Included above are illustrations developed from the work of Zaha Hadid, Robert Stern, Mario Botta, Paula Jackman, and Pancho Guedes.

Depth Cues in Orthographics

However, the most dramatic transformation of the elevation is made with the introduction of the apparent space of the pseudo-perspective. This is made possible by the insertion of a vanishing point at eye level on the plane of the elevation and by the resultant exploitation of the implied three-dimensional volume between elevation and viewer.

46

In linear form, these axonometric projections appear devoid of all depth cues apart from that of overlap, but they compel powerful sensations of space. This compulsion is in our mind's eye and results from its habit of seeing the parallelogram or rhombus as a rectangle occupying space--for even when all depth cues are absent, the parallelogram continues to retain spatial meaning.

For example, the rich quality of depth and space in this axonometric of an interior design for a shop, taken from the work of Eva Jiricna, relies not on shade and shadow but on an exclusive use of high contrast in value, texture, and pattern to differentiate between wall, floor, and unit finishes.

5

The projection of the plan into the nonconverging space of axonometrics produces a synthetic spatial world in which many architects examine the implications of their formal ideas. The cues of shade and shadow are often added in order to countermand the inherent distortion, such as in this "planometric" drawing taken from the work of Michael Stiff.

N.B.: The current interest in axonometrics in design recycles an earlier fascination in the 1920s when Modern Movement designers rejected perspective drawing as limited, finite, and closed. Axonometrics gained favor in the works of Theo van Doesburg and Le Corbusier, as they were seen to correspond to an "unequivocal representation of space."

Gallery of Alternative Drawing Types

Beyond the basic range of orthographics there is a series of drawing types that provide alternative viewing points or, when combined as composite graphics using two or more systems, allow hybrid vehicles for the communication of more complex or more spatially enhanced information. One such graphic combination unfolds the plan and elevation in direct relationship. In flattening the two, it provides a true-to-scale and simultaneous view of both horizontal and vertical planes.

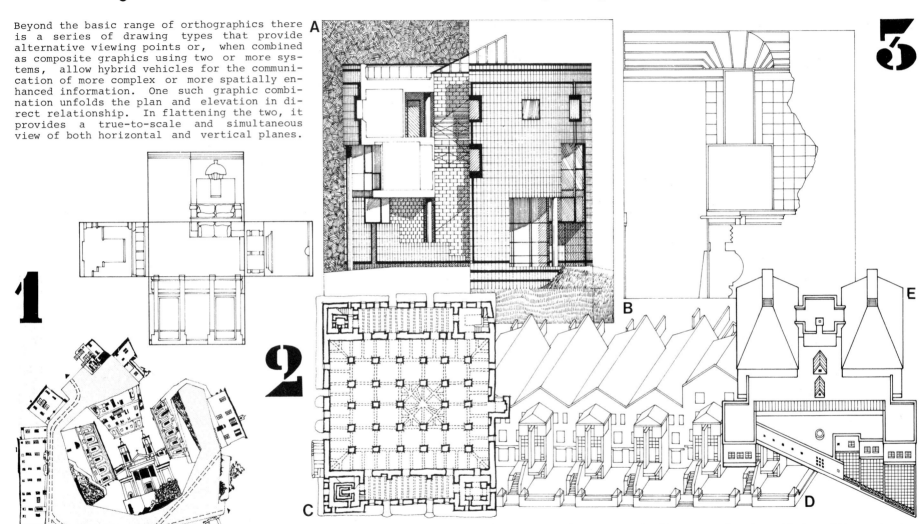

An unusual variation on this unfolding theme is found in the color restoration work of designer Giovanni Brino. In order to study the contextual relationship of facade colors in Turin's streets and piazzas, he flipped back elevations at 45 degrees to produce a montage of streetscapes.

The traditional section elevation combines a simultaneous drawing that splits exterior appearance with a view of interior elevations (A). Such graphics are generally associated with symmetrical forms. Interior wall elevations (B) are usually drawn by interior designers and visualized without their surrounding sectional cut for an exclusive concentration on internal events. More elaborate ceiling designs will call for a reflected ceiling plan (C). This version of the plan is true-to-scale and drawn as if viewed as the reflection in a continuously "mirrored" floor plane. One variation on the plan oblique (axonometric) is the elevation oblique (D), which simply substitutes a true plan for a true elevation, which is then projected back into the illusion of space at the same scale. Another variation involves the use of a true plan placed square-on, with the elevations projected vertically (E). The drawings are derived from the work of Rick Mather, Michael Graves, Jeremy Dixon, and John Tuomey.

Gallery of Alternative Drawing Types

The worm's-eye-view plan projection--commonly known as an "up-view" axonometric--flips the true-to-scale plan for a paraline projection drawing that provides the designer with an impossible vantage point that is located below the ground plane. The resultant graphic view gives simultaneous glimpses of exterior and interior wall planes together with a focus on the ceiling plane. This drawing is based on the work of James Stirling and Michael Wilford.

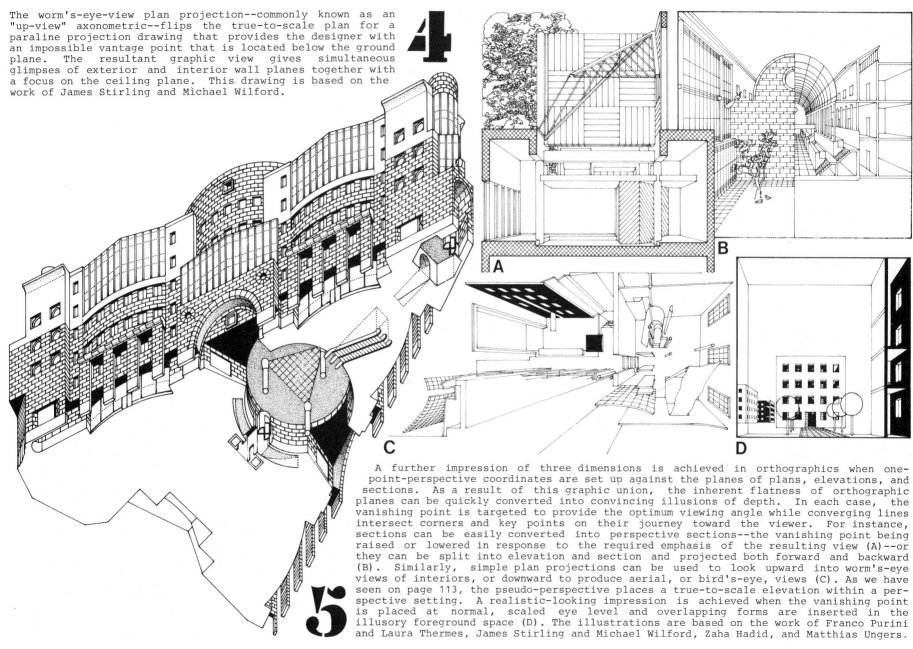

A further impression of three dimensions is achieved in orthographics when one-point-perspective coordinates are set up against the planes of plans, elevations, and sections. As a result of this graphic union, the inherent flatness of orthographic planes can be quickly converted into convincing illusions of depth. In each case, the vanishing point is targeted to provide the optimum viewing angle while converging lines intersect corners and key points on their journey toward the viewer. For instance, sections can be easily converted into perspective sections--the vanishing point being raised or lowered in response to the required emphasis of the resulting view (A)--or they can be split into elevation and section and projected both forward and backward (B). Similarly, simple plan projections can be used to look upward into worm's-eye views of interiors, or downward to produce aerial, or bird's-eye, views (C). As we have seen on page 113, the pseudo-perspective places a true-to-scale elevation within a perspective setting. A realistic-looking impression is achieved when the vanishing point is placed at normal, scaled eye level and overlapping forms are inserted in the illusory foreground space (D). The illustrations are based on the work of Franco Purini and Laura Thermes, James Stirling and Michael Wilford, Zaha Hadid, and Matthias Ungers.

Exploding, Cutting, and Dissolving Orthographics

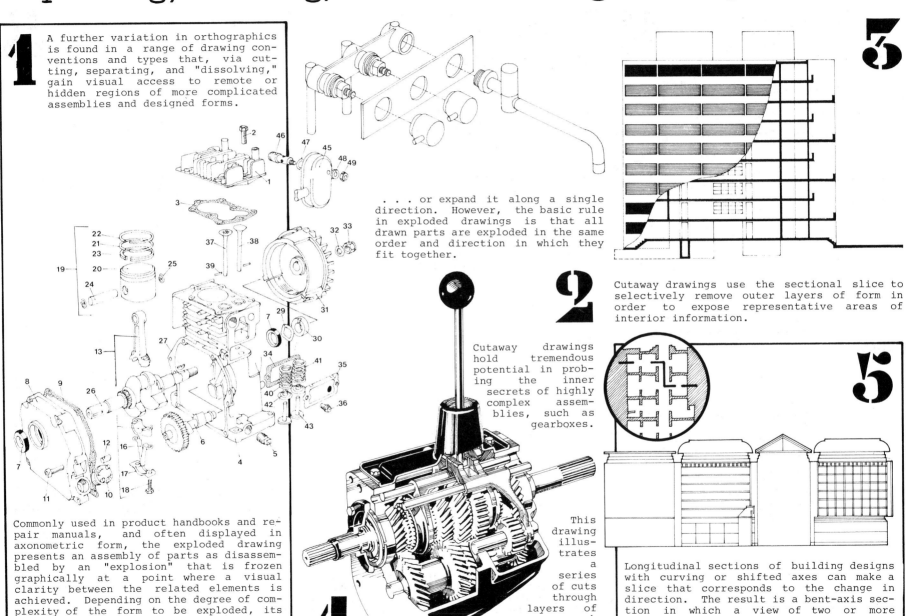

1 A further variation in orthographics is found in a range of drawing conventions and types that, via cutting, separating, and "dissolving," gain visual access to remote or hidden regions of more complicated assemblies and designed forms.

. . . or expand it along a single direction. However, the basic rule in exploded drawings is that all drawn parts are exploded in the same order and direction in which they fit together.

Commonly used in product handbooks and repair manuals, and often displayed in axonometric form, the exploded drawing presents an assembly of parts as disassembled by an "explosion" that is frozen graphically at a point where a visual clarity between the related elements is achieved. Depending on the degree of complexity of the form to be exploded, its drawn elements can stretch the space of their intervals multi-directionally . . .

2 Cutaway drawings hold tremendous potential in probing the inner secrets of highly complex assemblies, such as gearboxes.

This drawing illustrates a series of cuts through layers of space, each allowing a view through to the next.

3 Cutaway drawings use the sectional slice to selectively remove outer layers of form in order to expose representative areas of interior information.

5 Longitudinal sections of building designs with curving or shifted axes can make a slice that corresponds to the change in direction. The result is a bent-axis section in which a view of two or more sectioned planes are presented in a simultaneous fashion.

Exploding, Cutting, and Dissolving Orthographics

When applied to axonometrics, the slice of a section can easily travel in three dimensions and follow a predetermined route that best reveals the internal information to be exposed. However, as in all cutaway and sectioned graphics, both the trajectory and thickness of the incision should be clearly indicated.

Within this spatial convention, lines that are broken using short dashes or dots function as hidden lines and signify elements that occur behind the plane of a drawing. Conversely, long-dashed lines indicate elements that exist forward of the plane of the drawing. However, this language of orthographic depth is freely interpreted by designers, and dashed or lightly drawn lines tend to prevail. In this axonometric of a design for a studio and taken from the work of Edward Jones, both the sectional cut and the transparency of the broken line combine to allow an overall view of its interior. In this drawing the ghosted volume is complete, even down to the hidden lines of the side entrance recess and the detail of the front window.

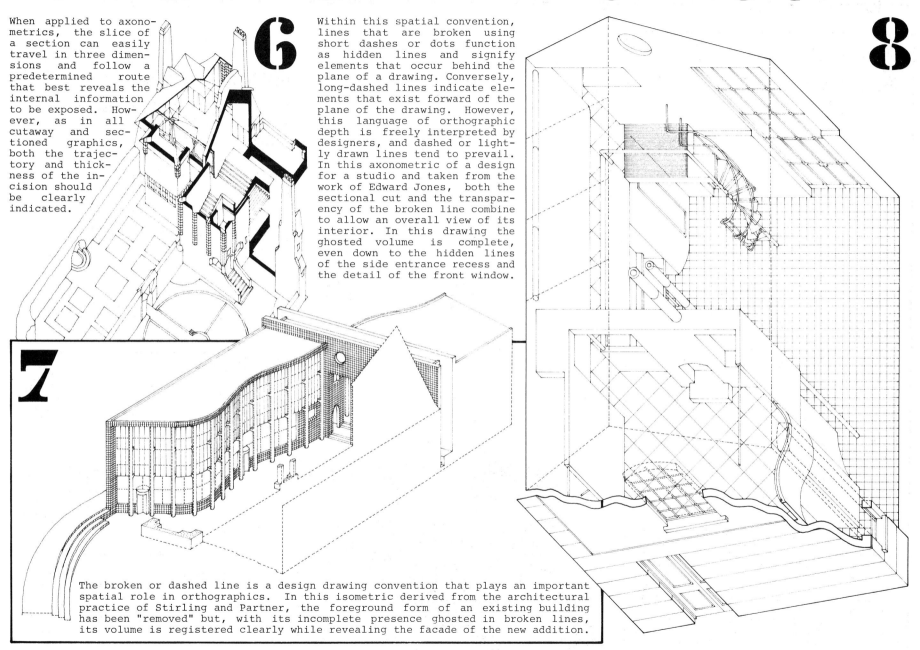

The broken or dashed line is a design drawing convention that plays an important spatial role in orthographics. In this isometric derived from the architectural practice of Stirling and Partner, the foreground form of an existing building has been "removed" but, with its incomplete presence ghosted in broken lines, its volume is registered clearly while revealing the facade of the new addition.

Multiview Design Drawings

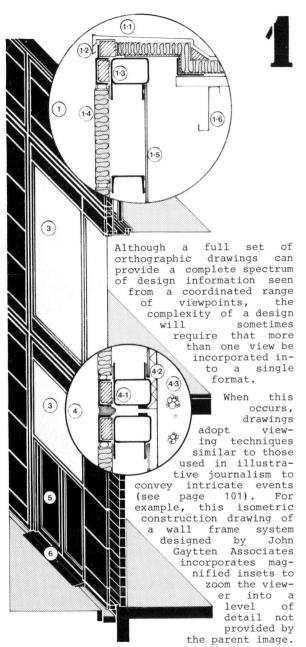

1

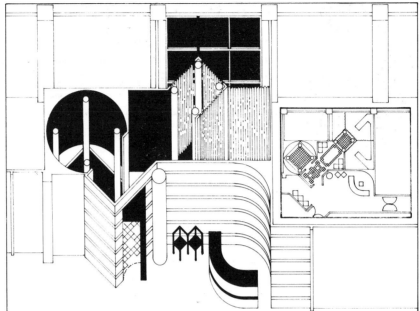

2

The use of insets to communicate aspects of related spatial information can be found in all forms of design drawing. Here, an axonometric incorporates its own plan as an integral part of its format in order to show the broader setting of its more selective projection. This design for a beauty salon was derived from the work of Patrick Dignan and Douglas Read.

Although a full set of orthographic drawings can provide a complete spectrum of design information seen from a coordinated range of viewpoints, the complexity of a design will sometimes require that more than one view be incorporated into a single format.

When this occurs, drawings adopt viewing techniques similar to those used in illustrative journalism to convey intricate events (see page 101). For example, this isometric construction drawing of a wall frame system designed by John Gaytten Associates incorporates magnified insets to zoom the viewer into a level of detail not provided by the parent image.

3

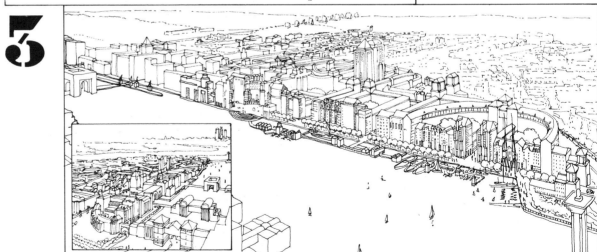

This perspective of a proposal for a River Thames dockside village by Form Design attempts to extend the directional confinement of its main aerial view by inserting an alternative glimpse within its frame of reference. This need for a second look taken from another vantage point represents the first step in the production of sequential perspectives that, when made at eye level, can take the viewer on a visual walk around the space of the designer's intentions.

6 IMAGE— BUILDING ISSUES

Time and Technique

1 Although they can be time-consuming, most design drawings are produced against pressing deadlines. Therefore, issues such as size, technique, medium, and the amount of information to be communicated become a serious consideration at the outset.

2 The selection of the rendering technique will also be affected by the available time-frame. Below are a range of basic value-creating techniques, each describing the same image and individually timed in the duration of their production.

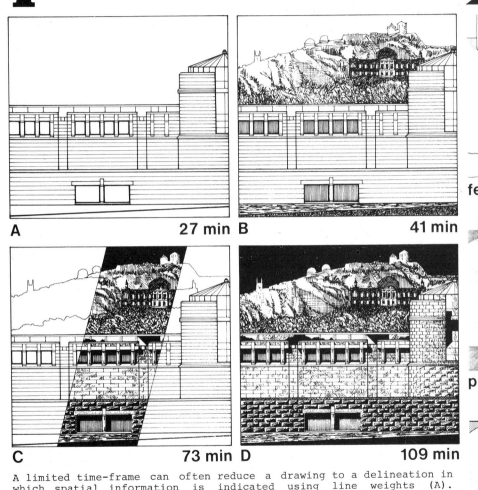

A   27 min   B   41 min

C   73 min   D   109 min

A limited time-frame can often reduce a drawing to a delineation in which spatial information is indicated using line weights (A). When time is pressing and more information is to be imparted, variations on the theme of selection can be adopted--for example, the employment of a precision drawing within the context of a freehand, rapid rendering (B), or the elaboration of detail or color in an isolated but clearly defined and representative area of the graphic (C). Longer time-spans will allow a greater indulgence in more complete renditions of a simulated reality using all the depth cues available (D). The drawings are based on the work of Arup Associates.

felt-tip wash   13 min

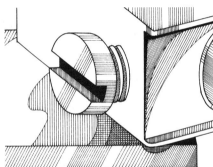

freehand hatching   20 min

pencil wash   26 min

ruled hatching   42 min

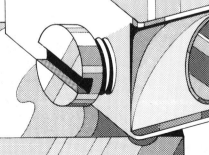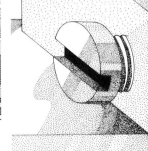

dry-transfer tone   57 min

freehand stippling   76 min

Time and Technique

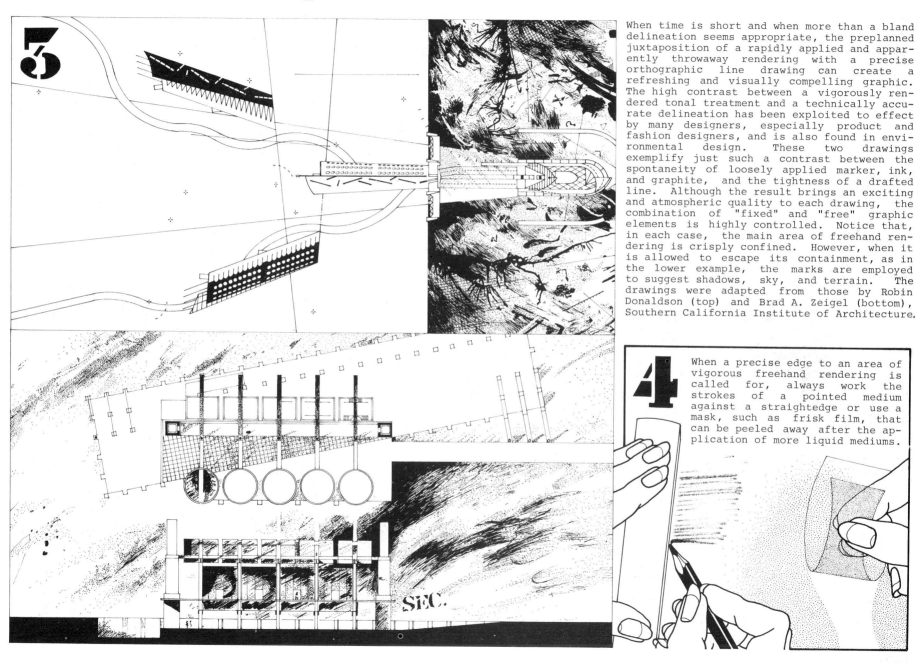

When time is short and when more than a bland delineation seems appropriate, the preplanned juxtaposition of a rapidly applied and apparently throwaway rendering with a precise orthographic line drawing can create a refreshing and visually compelling graphic. The high contrast between a vigorously rendered tonal treatment and a technically accurate delineation has been exploited to effect by many designers, especially product and fashion designers, and is also found in environmental design. These two drawings exemplify just such a contrast between the spontaneity of loosely applied marker, ink, and graphite, and the tightness of a drafted line. Although the result brings an exciting and atmospheric quality to each drawing, the combination of "fixed" and "free" graphic elements is highly controlled. Notice that, in each case, the main area of freehand rendering is crisply confined. However, when it is allowed to escape its containment, as in the lower example, the marks are employed to suggest shadows, sky, and terrain. The drawings were adapted from those by Robin Donaldson (top) and Brad A. Zeigel (bottom), Southern California Institute of Architecture.

When a precise edge to an area of vigorous freehand rendering is called for, always work the strokes of a pointed medium against a straightedge or use a mask, such as frisk film, that can be peeled away after the application of more liquid mediums.

Technique and Style

The style of a design drawing can often be inspired by the nature of its message. For instance, these two architectural drawings make an interesting comparison because they not only represent and reflect quite different time factors in their production, but also make references to drawing techniques and modes of representation not usually employed in orthographics.

The example on the left is based upon the superb draftings of Italian designers Franco Purini and Laura Thermes and was included in an exhibition of their conceptual design work. Their drawings function almost as essays in pen-and-ink rendering techniques, for their formats are crammed with a rich assortment of meticulously drawn and highly concentrated detail. This painstaking drawing employs a line and value structure that makes overt references to the qualities of old engravings, such as those by Piranesi. However, it is this simulation of the engraving technique that is entirely appropriate to the subject matter, i.e., an architectural scenario in which ancient fragments project above a collection of new ruins.

By contrast, the drawing above develops an elevation into the implied space of a pseudo-perspective. More interestingly, this drawing of a private house designed for a traditional setting in the Algarve, Portugal, also conveys the impression of a quickly drawn objective sketch, thereby imbuing the design proposal with an "I was there" feeling. Although the house was unbuilt at the time of drawing, this sketch cleverly converts the subjectivity of an orthographic into the conviction and technique of a freehand objective drawing. Drawing based on an example of the work of Michael Brown Associates.

Drawing Size, Distance, and Reproduction

1

Graphite Grades	Ft	M
4H	2	0.6
2H	4	1.3
HB	7	2.0
2B	9	2.7
4B	11	3.4

Technical Pen Nibs		
0.18	3	0.9
0.25	4	1.2
0.35	5	1.5
0.5	7	2.0
0.7	8	2.5

A factor that will also affect the adopted form of drawing technique is the size of the image. The issue of size will depend upon the scale of complexity of the drawing content and upon the selected mode of presentation--the latter decision being governed by the nature of the intended audience. If a drawing is to be produced at a large scale for presentation to a panel of viewers, the intensities of line and value have to be adjusted so that they match the distance over which the drawing is viewed. Failure to increase the boldness of ink line weights and graphite grades over extended viewing distances will, inevitably, cause a breakdown in communication. For instance, this table illustrates a maximum viewing distance for each of the ink line weights and graphite grades shown.

2

Design drawings are proliferated by several reproduction processes including diazo, photocopying (xeroxography), and photography. Photocopying is a common means of rapid resizing and reproduction, and is used especially for the transfer of line drawings made on thinner and translucent materials to surfaces that will accept a wider range of rendering treatments. Also widely used is diazo printing, a process that involves the passage of light through a drawing and relies totally on originals being worked on transparent materials. In turn, techniques for creating value on such drawings have to be transparent--tonal ranges resulting from the amount of light that is filtered by variation in the intensity of application. Such tonal treatments are frequently applied to the reverse side of the drawing to avoid damaging the original linework. Here are just a few of the rendering mediums and techniques that are conducive to diazo printing:

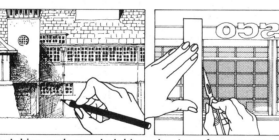

hatching and cross-hatching in pen and in pencil **dry-transfer screens**

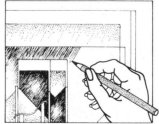

colored pencils and markers (colors are printed as values)

cotton-wool-applied graphite dust (collected from a pointer)

3

Drawings will often be drastically reduced in size for use as illustrations in reports and brochures, and also for publication in magazines. Three basic issues are important when drawing for reduction. First, use ink and not pencil. Second, avoid very fine lines, as these are susceptible to erosion when subject to reduction. Third, the allowance made for intervals between lines in hatching is critical because, if too close, they tend to fill in when reduced. The basic rules are: The larger the reduction, the wider the spacing between lines; never draw lines with less than their own thickness as interval between them, and work to a minimum line thickness in the final reduction of 0.1 mm.

Format and Frame of Reference

Another decision concerns the nature of the frame of reference, i.e., the shape of the drawing in relation to the outer edge of the drawing paper. Essentially, the picture frame functions as a window that separates the drawn illusion from the sheet, and through which the space of the image is viewed. As if to complement the shape of the periphery of our visual field, some designers will abandon the traditional rectangle or square and work within circular or elliptical formats, such as this isometric in a circle from the work of Herman Hertzberger. However, when a strong and rendered illusion of space is required, such drawings should be worked on smooth paper so that any surface grain will not optically invade the image and negate its illusion of depth.

2 There are degrees of departure from the formality of delineated, geometrical formats. For instance, rather than be bounded by a line, frames can be suggested with an invisible boundary that is assumed and "painted in" by the eye.

The sketchlike spontaneity of irregular frames of reference is common but--in order not to weaken the pictorial illusion--they should be carefully shaped in relation to the spatial structure of the drawing they define, as in this example based on the work of Robert Stern.

This drawing from a perspective by Frank Lloyd Wright shows two methods of creating more dynamic formats. On its left side, elements from within the implied space of the courtyard are allowed to break through the confines of the rectangular frame and occupy a space forward of the picture plane. Further, the lower edge of the format is formed by the negative silhouette of foreground foliage.

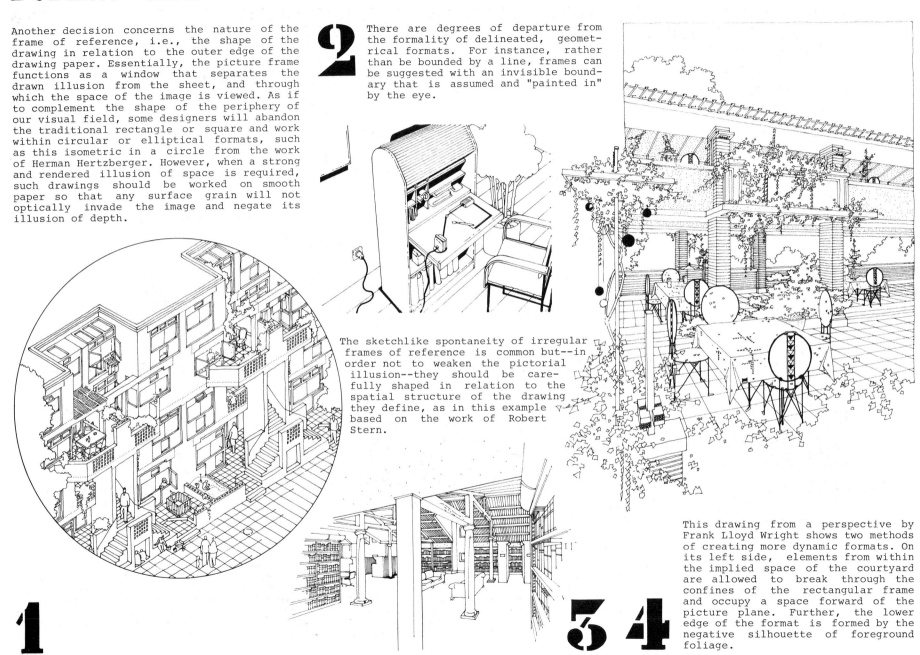

1

3 4

Format and Frame of Reference

This drawing is a perspective from a design for a private residence by Bolivia's leading architect, Juan Carlos Calderón. It plays a game with its frame similar to that shown in frame 4. This is because its center of attention, i.e., the building, appears to sit forward of its framed backdrop to occupy an illusory space located between the viewer and the picture plane. This illusion is reinforced by the manner in which foreground elements apparently oversail and overlap the stylized confinement of their context. At the same time, the backdrop disconnects itself from the building, only to be eroded by the drifting smoke--a graphic device that functions to reconnect the building with the surrounding space of the picture plane. This graphic game with the frame of reference induces a stagelike quality that possibly derives from its author's involvement in the creation of several opera set designs in his native country.

125

Message Areas: Orthographics

When we compare the amount of time spent in producing drawings with the time spent in viewing them, it becomes important that the central message of a graphic be clear at the outset of image-building. This consideration will affect the nature of the message area. When considering the central message, we should remember that the basic function of the eye is to detect movement and change in the field of vision. When the stimulus is graphic, the eye is immediately attracted to the region of greater contrast.

The harnessing of contrast to the area of the message is shown in this site plan from a drawing by Kisho Kurokawa. Here, the dramatic change in line type, the localized use of value, and the projection of shadows exclusive to the building sharply etch the footprint of the architectural intention.

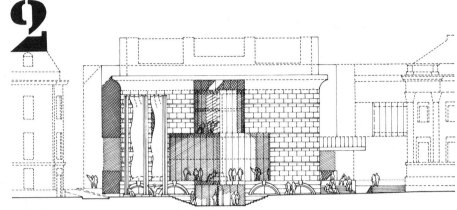

2

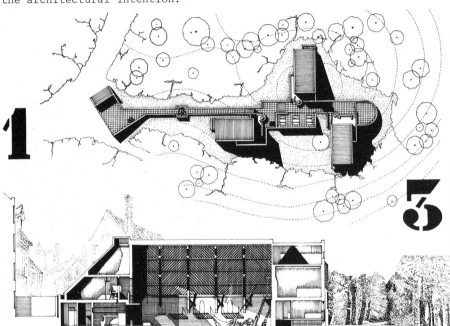

1

However, the employment of change in technique to attract and inform can entertain varying degrees of contrast. A more subtle visual signal is revealed in this elevation of an extension to London's National Gallery by Stirling, Wilford, & Associates. The proposed facade is portrayed with unbroken lines and appears complete with modules of building materials, shadows, and visitors, while the sky-line massing and fenestration of its immediate context are ghosted in dashed lines.

3

A switch in ink rendering techniques between the ruled hatching on interior cells of this section and the freehand treatment of nearby trees and houses is further emphasized by the two kinds of graphic space portrayed. One is the diminishing depth of the perspective setting; the other the dimensionless depth of the section and its end wall elevation, which enlists shadows and light variation to imply a sensation of space. Therefore, the difference in drawing mode, drawing technique—separated by the abstraction of the sectional cut—attracts the eye to the main event, i.e., the spotlit stage. Drawing based on one by K. Kontozoglou for Tim Ronalds Architects.

4

Paraline drawings exert their own visual pull—the projection of "pop-up" forms from the base plane creating an irresistible attraction for the eye. Message areas in axonometrics and isometrics become intensified when surface grain, shade, and shadow are applied to vertical and/or horizontal planes of projected forms. Meanwhile, contextual information is often left in plan to emphasize the message area, or, if projected, is usually confined to a simple, contrasting delineation. The illustration is based on a detail of a drawing by Jack Sloan with Nicholl, Page, & Park.

Message Areas: Perspectives

When a building design is the main message of a perspective drawing (or an orthographic drawing), it can utilize a contrast in levels of detail and a variation in drawing technique to attract attention. For instance, the stark contrast between detailed fenestration and blank, delineated landscaping in this perspective of a new office building from the Alec French Partnership leaves the viewer in no doubt about its message. However, this drawing conveys a second, more subtle message. This stems from the dashed-line mass, which offers us a comparison between the proposed design and the ghost of the building it intends to replace.

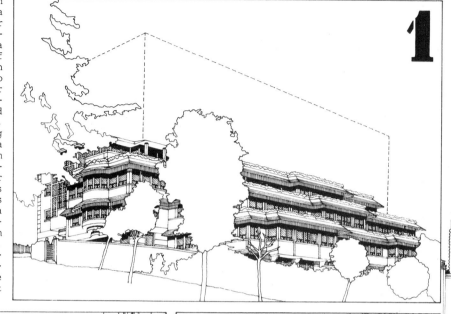

However, as the main function of the perspective is to test the three-dimensional implications of a design, it is not always the case that the proposed architecture becomes the center of attention. When appropriateness to surroundings is the central issue, angles of perspective, together with a nonselective rendition, can illustrate a proposed intervention as an integrated and less obvious facet of architectural space. The above drawings are based on "before" and "after" perspectives of a proposed addition to London's Royal Opera House from the practice of Jeremy Dixon in conjunction with the Building Design Partnership.

A common means of focusing the eye on the message area is to target the vanishing point within or near the zone to be occupied by the design. When you direct the lines of convergence that describe planes and events seen parallel to the angle of view, you steer the eye straight toward the center of attention. Furthermore, in order to emphasize the message when depicting tall buildings, as in this scheme by Terry Farrell, you can raise eye levels to achieve a maximum exposure.

Compositional Hints: One-Point Perspective

1 The creation of more visually interesting perspectives relies upon a series of basic compositional rules, which, being intended to help the beginner, are reviewed over the following five pages.

2

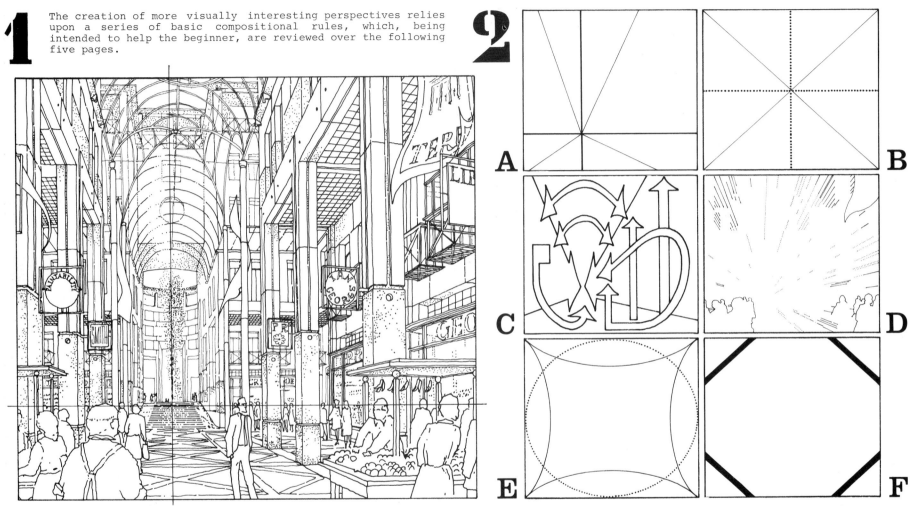

A basic tip is to avoid placing the vanishing point at the very center of the drawing format. This is because such a location tends to lead the eye directly to the heart of symmetrical compositions. In this interior perspective of a design for a colonnaded fruit and vegetable market from one by Robert Thompson for the practice of Richard MacCormac, notice that the vanishing point-- and its attendant focal point--is located off-center and toward the lower left region of the format.

This off-center positioning of perspective coordinates avoids the predictability of a symmetrical arrangement (A), and also negates the danger of vertical or horizontal elements or forces that might fragment the format into the static dullness of four equal units (B). Remember that each line, edge, and positive or negative shape in a composition will act as a visual pointer to the eye as it journeys around the space of a drawing (C). Therefore, another important tip is to make sure that the lines of convergence in perspectives do not coincide with the corners of frames; if they do, they might encourage the eye to evacuate the composition (D). The corners of rectangular formats are sensitive graphic zones and should be handled with care. This is because they represent regions of potential distortion that lie outside our natural and elliptically shaped visual field (E). As if to compensate for this distortion, many designers insert corner "stops," i.e., positive or negative shapes that keep the eye within the format (F).

Compositional Hints: One-Point Perspective

If we return to our perspective example on the facing page and examine the four corners of its format, we see how the two lower corners, together with the one on the upper right, have been modified with directional elements that are incidental to the architecture but aim to keep the eye circulating within the format. Also, so as not to draw the eye from the center of attention, they are suggested rather than detailed.

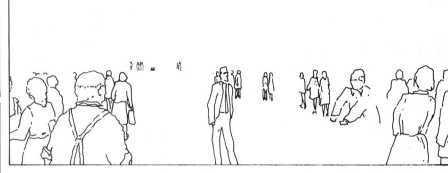

If we now isolate the figures from the perspective drawing, we also learn something about their function. For instance, instead of being inserted casually as isolated elements, the figures are structured into overlapping groups that, in coinciding with our given angle of view, both animate the architectural space and exploit its depth and change in level (see pages 139-141).

Finally, if we separate the raw architectural perspective construction from its entourage (figures, stalls, signage, banners, etc.) and its tonal rendering--albeit minimal--we begin to understand the difference between a potentially stark mechanical perspective and one filled with light and activity. This analysis also demonstrates how a series of secondary focal points is designed to surround and intensify an off-center message area.

Visual Interest: Two-Point Perspective

This is another drawing--this time a two-point perspective--based on one by Robert Thompson for the design practice of Richard MacCormac. It shows the main entrance to the proposed design for a fruit and vegetable market hall. Although this perspective breaks some of the basic compositional rules (and such rules were made to be broken), it can teach us something about constructing more dynamic compositions.

Visual Interest: Two-Point Perspective

2

When foreground trees are added, they occupy dramatic and irregular positioning. They function to subframe the format into three differing volumes of negative space, with the message area being viewed through the middle. However, its location is left of center of the picture format, but right of center between the trees. Thus, by avoiding a static duality, an entire sequence of slightly eccentric displacements creates a fascinating dynamic.

3

If we reduce this perspective to its basic two-point structure, we see that its center of gravity--represented by the eye level and the main message area (the entrance to the market hall)--occupies a point in the format that is lower left of dead center. This eccentric location also causes greater disparity between the negative shapes of sky mass and courtyard space--and therefore more visual interest.

4

5

Again, notice the function of corner "stops"--the two upper corners being softened by the modifying effect of arched negative space caused by the curve of branches and foliage. Further, the lower right-hand corner is literally "stopped" by a positive form, thus arresting the rhythm of the railing that makes its entry in the lower left-hand corner.

As the left-hand side of formats represents the region from which the scanning eye usually makes its entrance into a graphic, it is important that this area not be visually blocked. However, the potential closure of this zone by the two trees on the extreme left is compensated for by the upward and inward sweep of the plane of the railing, which acts to direct the eye into the foreground space and toward the message area.

131

Visual Interest: Two-Point Perspective

The potential stifling of the left-hand side of the format is further compensated for by the counterbalancing emphasis caused by the contrast of a minimal tonal rendering and an extra richness of line intensity that draws attention to the right-hand portion. Another feature of this contrasting area is its shape, which, apart from framing and pointing to the message area, also assumes an elliptical outer edge. In reflecting the shape of our visual field, this edge encourages the eye up, over, and down into the heart of the composition.

7

6

Indeed, this area of increased visual weight and contrast--together with the shape and location of unrendered foliage, and the position of both figures and railing--functions to surround the center of attention with an eccentrically orbiting cluster of secondary focal points.

However, additional figures and trees are scattered throughout this perspective. Apart from those occupying the foreground and background of the courtyard, other figures peer from windows and, together with trees and shrubs, appear on balconies to animate both the horizontal and vertical layers of space within the drawing.

8

It is important to note that the eye finds the clustering of like objects, such as trees and figures, to be more visually fascinating when grouped in odd rather than even numbers. For instance, notice the insertion of three foreground and three background figures, and the introduction of five large trees.

9

Trees in Perspectives

 1 As we have seen, trees can play important roles in perspective compositions. However, when they are in the company of buildings, they should be incorporated and rendered with care.

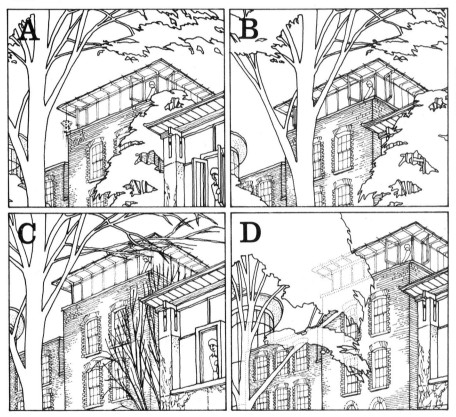

For example if we examine the upper section of the perspective on page 130, we find that the arrangement of tree branches and foliage has been designed to remain clear of all critical corners and edges of the buildings beyond (A). This is because junctions of form and the corners of planes are used by the eye to complete its "painting in" of shape recognition. Therefore, even when a tree structure and a building mass are directly superimposed, it is important that a glimpse of these reference points be maintained (B). Any survey of architectural perspectives will discover other devices for maintaining the continuity of important building silhouettes. Some drawings will depict their information in a winter setting so as to filter, rather than obscure, the outline of mass (C). Other drawings will use the graphic convention of an X-ray view through a dissolved mass of foliage to an indication of the shape of the form behind (D).

2 When a change in ground plane level is not present in perspectives, trees, unlike the stature differential of adult figures, can be made to vary in height in order to exploit a greater visual interest. This degree of interest is heightened if, rather than define planes parallel to the picture plane, they describe planes that converge into the space of the drawing. Furthermore, if they describe an irregular sequence and thereby create a dissimilar pattern of negative space, visual interest is again enhanced. This illustration depicts a detail from a drawing by John Bradbury.

3 Therefore, a basic rule when designing compositions is to exploit a variation in order, rhythm, and pattern whenever possible. In so doing, we exploit the implied space of a perspective. When we use trees to emphasize depth, we should draw them with integrity, i.e., from a source of reference. Also, when rendering them in detail, we should remember their near and far spatial appearance, as shown in this drawing based on the work of the Building Design Partnership.

133

Learning from Photographs: Composition

1

2

Recomposed photograph formats can easily be sought and isolated using the expandable and contractible L-shaped viewfinder described on page 73.

Once you have isolated a likely composition, either crop it from the photograph or mask it with a frame of white paper. Then place it alongside your drawing board and proceed to outline its major forms in pencil. If your photo-composition source is small, it is important that you increase the size of your drawing so that an inhibition of subsequent drawing techniques is avoided.

3

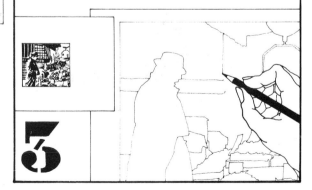

Although still viewed with suspicion by many, working from photographs as drawing sources can prove beneficial to beginners. Photographic references become useful especially when lack of time or accessibility makes an objective drawing of an actual reference impracticable. Also, drawing from photographs is in itself a useful activity, affording a singular concentration on content, drawing technique, and composition. The following exercise is one that, apart from reinforcing a contact with the appearance of things, aims to develop an eye for composition.

The first step involves the selection of a photograph that offers a richness of detail and a variety of form within its composition. The next step is to explore its format for a recomposed image that interests you enough to act as the source of your drawing. A good composition may contain a whole sequence of subcompositions that are generated by the framed isolation of its major and subordinate focal points. For instance, this series of compositions has been extracted from the parent image above.

Learning from Photographs: Composition

4 Once you have recorded the main formal structure, make a study of the main values. These can be assessed by overlaying the photograph with a thin sheet of tracing paper.

5 This overlay filters out all the superficial values for a concentration on those crucial to the main structure of the image. Now trace an outline around the visible areas of value.

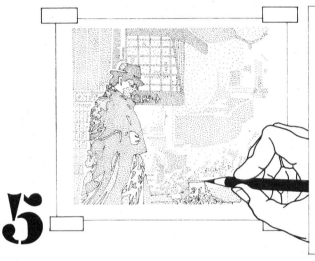

6 You have now produced a pattern that --once removed from the photograph-- will serve as a guide to the arrangement of value in the ensuing drawing.

7 After delineating the value pattern in pencil in the drawing, begin penwork around the center of interest using a technique of shading that is either suggested by the appearance of value in the photograph or drawn from one of those shown on pages 56-57.

8 "Artist's license" is a term that describes your decision about which features of the photograph to dramatize in the drawing, and which features to suppress. This decision develops a selectivity that is a basic compositional skill.

9 Furthermore, the same skill is exercised when you decide the way in which the center of interest is developed outward toward the picture's edge. For example, those parts of the image that you decide to elaborate, and those parts you leave blank, will respond to your sense of compositional design.

Learning from Photographs: Light

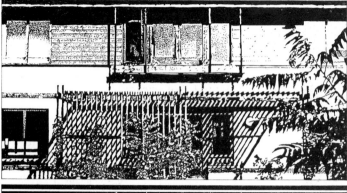

The most important ingredient in our understanding of space is the quality and direction of light. Although its constantly shifting behavior on form and surface will be experienced in objective drawing and sketching, a good method of further realizing its pictorial depiction is to work from photographs. For instance, the issue of direction of light is critical in composition, as it is a decision that will reflect the need to illuminate those planes you wish to stress. Therefore, in using a photograph in which light enters from the right, this drawing exercise attempts to predict the effect of an alternative structure of light and value when the same stark sunlight is allowed to enter from the left.

2

Another useful exercise is to modify graphically the light quality in a photograph of a facade from its daytime impression to one of representing a nighttime experience. This transformation can be an enlightening experience, as the conceptual switch from sunlight to electric light will cause mass to dissolve and window apertures to glow in a dramatic positive-negative reversal of the source image.

3

The fine-tuning of graduated ink line rendering techniques, which will account for the subtle modulations of daylight and electric light that illuminate a variety of finishes on vertical and horizontal surfaces, is yet another way that the study of photographs can enhance your drawing prowess.

Rendering Light in Perspectives

In pure line drawings, light can be hinted at by using variation in line weights--a thicker line describing the side of objects in shade. Also, its diffusion can be simulated by using broken lines at points of strong illumination. Drawings such as this one, based on a detail of the work of Carlo Mollino, literally delineate the direction of rays of light in a positive manner.

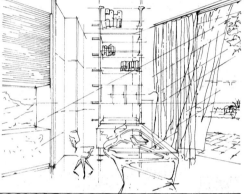

1 Many designers who are known for their graphics have evolved highly personal and distinctive value-rendering techniques that are applied to emphasize the modulation of light in the space of their designs. However, in depicting light negatively, i.e., as a result of describing shade and shadow, these techniques must be flexible enough to indicate the subtle gradations of tone at different scales.

2

3 The convention of drawing light rays in line can also be seen in this detail taken from a reversed drawing by Roomet Aring. Here, the deployment of white lines on a black background is guided by the vanishing point to create a scintillating explosion of light that selectively etches the shape, and diffuses the edges, of objects and planes.

4 In this detail based on one of the superb ink renderings of Paul Rudolph, the linear graphic convention that suggests directional rays of light in line is elevated to an art form. Notice that the shimmering quality of light in this interior is achieved entirely with straightedge hatching and cross-hatching.

The Overlay Technique

1 The overlay technique is the most useful method of rapidly evolving all forms of design drawing. The technique begins with a basic draft of the required drawing, which is then moved onto a transparent overlay sheet by trace-transferring all the acceptable elements from the underlay original. This process of refinement--which leaves behind redundant and incorrect elements on the underlay--can continue ad infinitum from one surface to another until the final and acceptable drawing is achieved.

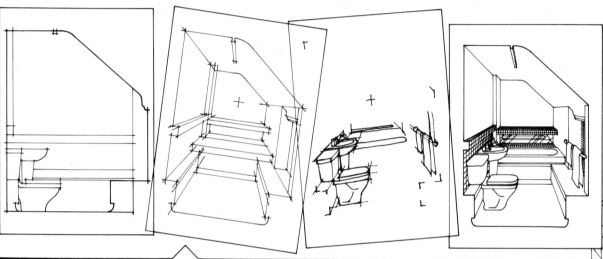

3 Yet another function of this technique is the rapid origination of perspectives on tracing paper. The drawing is achieved by overlaying the tracing paper on one of the range of proprietary grid sheets whose guiding coordinates offer a choice of eye-level views in both one- and two-point perspective. If required, the final tracing-paper drawing can then be transformed onto opaque board for rendering via the diazo or photocopy reproduction process.

N.B.: To avoid erasure of drafting errors in the overlay technique, work initial drawing stages in nonrepro blue pencil. These are then selectively overworked in pen--the ink line only being printed by any subsequent reproduction.

2 This process of selective extraction also allows for the transformation of drawings into other mediums, techniques, and drawing styles. For instance, a common conversion is that of a precise and technically drafted orthographic or perspective into a more sensuous-appearing freehand line drawing. The ultimate freehand drawing is produced with confidence--its freshness remaining dimensionally informed by the precision of the underlay.

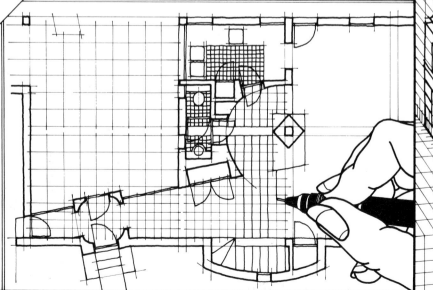

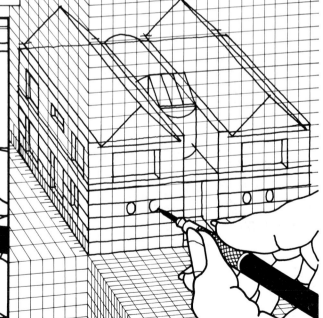

The Overlay Technique

Perspective drawings are often ruined by weakly drawn or stereotyped entourage elements, such as human figures and trees, etc. This is caused when the contrast between the lines describing man-made planes and those describing organic elements is heightened by introducing the latter in an uncaring manner. Therefore, when figures are introduced to bring scale and life to a drawing, it is crucial--especially if they are to occupy important pictorial zones--that they be derived from accurate sources of reference.

If you hit problems when trying to produce convincingly populated perspectives, the potential of the overlay technique can come to your rescue. This is because--providing that it is in the appropriate scale and perspective--it allows any visual reference material to be slipped beneath the overlay sheet for its traced integration into the composition. This illustration is based on the work of D.E.G.W.

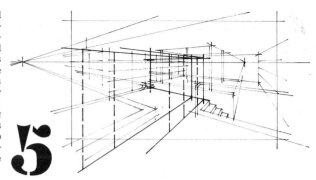

For example, a fast method of correctly locating figures in perspectives is to first mark off the height of an average figure on the vertical scale and project it out into the foreground zone toward and through the points to be occupied (if there are several points to be occupied across the foreground zone, then lines should be projected into each of the zones). A vertical line drawn to connect the projected lines will find the height of a figure at any given point between foreground and background.

The vertical height lines of figures can now be used to guide the insertion of photographs of people cut from magazines. Avoid isolating them as individuals, but group them using overlap to encourage a sense of depth. However, if the found photographic images are out of scale with the perspective, these can be resized using the reduction or enlargement capability of a photocopier. The reduction or enlargement ratio is simply found by dividing the required height of the figure by the actual height of its photographic counterpart.

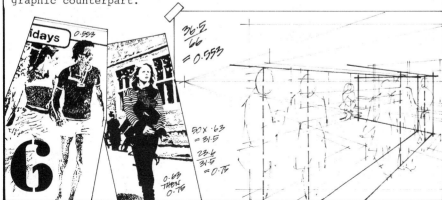

Once all the figures have been satisfactorily located on the perspective drawing, overlay a sheet of transparent paper and begin tracing the final version of the image with confidence. Begin by tracing the foreground figures before working on those in the middleground. Continue working from the front to the back of the perspective--including all the other information as you go--until, finally, you reach the background.

Figures in Perspectives

Though figures in value-rendered drawings can be represented in the same tonal technique, so as to ensure that their pictorial existence does not compromise the impact of their setting, they are often kept as simple outline drawings. Whichever the case, however, their incorporation into graphic space should, through a modification of their detailed depiction, recognize the effect of distance.

1

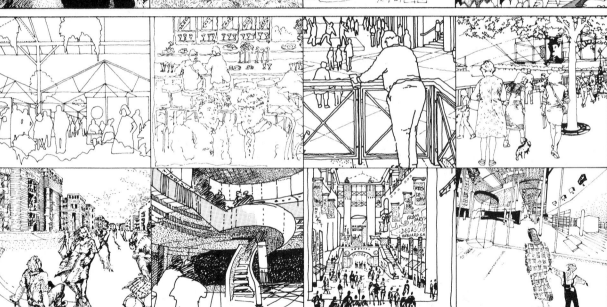

2

In fully rendered perspectives, value-rendered figures appear less detached from their surroundings than do their delineated counterparts. However, even when positioned in the foreground, they should be shown simply and in a manner that extends the technique employed for the drawing as a whole.

4

3

While maintaining the integrity of human figures, many designers develop a personal style for their appearance in perspectives. Common mistakes to avoid when inserting figures include symmetrical posture and static grouping. Also, their presence should be used to describe an animated interaction with the objects and space of their setting without obscuring or diminishing the central message of the drawing. The illustrations above are based on the work of the Cambridge Seven Associates, Sebrire & Allsopp, M.E.P.C., De Blacam & Meagher, Robert Thompson, Avery Associates, Rob Krier, John Melvin & Partners, Terry Farrell, and the Wilson Partnership.

Figures in Perspectives

This interior perspective of a design for a supermarket was drawn by Philip Jones, a fourth-year interior design student at the Middlesex Polytechnic. Using the overlay method, Philip used found photographic source figures to indicate activities that are appropriate to the setting. Notice that stiff, upright figures and hyperactive groups have been avoided, and that the figures' placement in the composition attempts to indicate spatial depth. The drawing was evolved in two stages. First, a preparatory perspective was constructed against a grid and developed until all the required information was incorporated. The second stage evolved as a selective, refined, and rendered overlay version of the first, but worked on translucent detail paper. White gouache was used to create the modeling on columns and create the reflective floor surface. Meanwhile, in conjunction with 2H and 2B graphite leads, a white pencil was used to pick out the space-frame roof structure. The figures were rendered in colored pencil. Finally, the drawing was bonded to a gray mat board--the detail paper support allowing its grayness to take part in the final impression.

Found-Image and Drawing Combinations

Composite perspectives can be quickly constructed from the assembly of found images and drawings. For example, this well-known graphic--adapted from the work of Aldo Rossi--fuses a line and hatched perspective drawing with a backcloth created from an engraving of trees and rock formations. The result is convincing--the mechanical hatching of shade and shadows on the architectural form being completely in sympathy with the texture of engraved foliage. To complete the spatial illusion, Rossi has also introduced starkly drawn shadows, cast from the stilted forms, to trace the contours of the foreground plane.

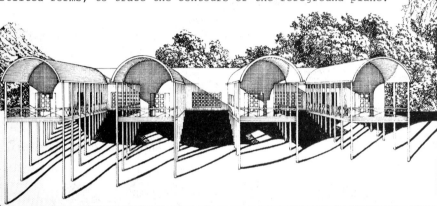

The insertion of found photographic elements into the foregrounds, middlegrounds, and backgrounds of perspective drawings is a fast and efficient means of assembling convincing graphics. Occasionally, this technique of image-building demands that a number of the found graphic components be resized in order to achieve their scaled fusion with the parent image. Resizing can be done instantly on a photocopier--the same reprographic process also being used to transform the completed original into the final fusion of a second-stage photocopied print.

This combination of an engraving with a line drawing is adapted from the work of Leon Krier. It makes an interesting comparison with Rossi's because, here, an engraving is used to provide a dramatic foreground space as a contextual setting for a building design. However, there is a further development in this composite image that is worth noting. A greater fusion of the two elements has been encouraged by the insertion of a group of drawn figures clad in modern dress who now occupy the street space with their engraved and period-costumed counterparts. Also, in the background zone, and behind the message area, further contextual buildings have been included that echo--both in design and drawing technique--those in the engraved foreground.

Drawing-Photograph Combinations

A further stage in the combination of drawings with other graphic material is represented by this image, which integrates a delineated perspective drawing of a proposed building design with a montage of photographic prints of the site.

Shot in panoramic sequence, the photographs document a riverside setting for a new office building designed by Darbourne & Darke, and produced as part of their successful submission to an invited competition. Notice that unwanted areas of the photograph have been removed to make way for the drawing and also to simulate the screening effect of proposed landscaping. Furthermore, a small group of drawn figures has been allowed to occupy the riverside walk, encouraging a greater fusion between the two graphic elements.

The process of integrating site photographs with drawings is fast and effective. Once the prints are assembled to complete the panorama, unwanted areas are cut away; then the prints are glued onto the finished line drawing. An alternative method is to first glue-assemble the prints intact to receive a direct application of the shaped and drawn elements. Perspective coordinates that guide the line drawing are established from the photographs by tracing the lines of convergence and locating the vanishing points (see pages 38–39). The line drawing is then worked on a tracing paper overlay and, once visually integrated with the photographic elements, is finally transferred into a composite form via photocopying or photography.

In simulating the tonal quality, light direction, and textural grain of its parent site photograph, the drawing technique of this building design attempts a closer visual match with the print of its intended setting. The quest for higher levels of reality in this instance stems, possibly, from the fact that what its designers, Saunders Boston, propose is a new college facility in the historic and highly sensitive campus at Cambridge University, England.

143

Index